MAJOR TRENDS IN
AMERICAN CHURCH HISTORY

MAJOR TRENDS IN AMERICAN CHURCH HISTORY

by

FRANCIS X. CURRAN, S.J.
Weston College, Weston, Mass.

THE AMERICA PRESS
NEW YORK

IMPRIMI POTEST

JAMES P. SWEENEY, S.J.

PROVINCIAL: NEW YORK PROVINCE

NIHIL OBSTAT

CENSOR DEPUTATUS

IMPRIMATUR

✠ FRANCIS J. SPELLMAN, D.D.

ARCHBISHOP OF NEW YORK

PRINTED IN THE UNITED STATES OF AMERICA
BY J. J. LITTLE & IVES COMPANY, NEW YORK

To My Mother

TABLE OF CONTENTS

INTRODUCTION

THE average American lives in complete ignorance of the religious history of his country. It is a lamentable fact that knowledge of this most important field of the history of the United States is restricted to but a few specialists.

One reason which may be adduced to explain this almost universal ignorance is the scarcity of studies treating the history of the Christian churches in the United States. Many chronicles of American religions, it is true, have been published.[1] But the overwhelming majority of these books are antiquated accounts of individual churches or denominations. In the past, church historians, both Catholic and Protestant, have manifested a singular lack of interest in the history of any church or sect save that of their own particular denominations. This trait is more pronounced among the Catholics. For while a few Protestant historians have published general histories of Christianity in the United States, no Catholic has ever undertaken the task. Even the chronicles of Catholicism have been neglected. In the last forty years but one general history of the Catholic Church in the United States has been published.

Consequently, the writer who would essay the construction from secondary sources of an outline of the history of American Christianity is confronted with difficulties. Gen-

[1] Cf. the lists in Case, Shirley J. *et al., Bibliography of the History of Christianity* and Mode, Peter G., *Source Book and Bibliographical Guide for American Church History.*

eralizations drawn from the histories of the individual churches or sects would be as enlightening as conclusions about the political history of the United States derived from the chronicles of the individual States.

A few authors have, nevertheless, attempted historical interpretations of our Christianity. Probably the most profound is Hall's *Religious Background of American Culture,* a study which, as indicated by its title, is more concerned with the effect of religion on the United States than the impact of the American environment on Christianity. Rowe's *History of Religion in the United States* finds significance in the progressive religious emancipation of the American people from the institutionalism and traditions of the Old World.[2] This emancipation, it is asserted, came about in three phases, the first of which saw the rejection of the authority of the State churches; the second, the abandonment of formal worship and preaching; the third, the jettisoning of the traditional doctrines of Protestant orthodoxy. Platner, in the *Religious History of New England,* mentions a theory which emphasizes three major periods of the history of Christianity in America: the metaphysical, the ethical and the aesthetic.[3]

These generalizations are, apparently, insufficiently general. They express, at most, tendencies in American Protestantism, which comprises, if one trusts the United States Religious Census for 1936, about fifty-five per cent of the total church membership of the nation. According to that census, the adherents of Protestantism, defined in the

[2] Rowe, Henry K., *History of Religion in the United States,* pp. vii, viii.
[3] Platner, John W. *et al., Religious History of New England,* p. 71.

widest sense, totaled about 31,000,000. In that number are included several large groups unacceptable as Protestants by many Protestant sects. But to these groups, with the omission of non-Christians, Eastern Orthodox and Old Catholics, may be applied the common definition of the term "Protestant" as given by Silcox and Fisher: "Sometimes, indeed, it seems that the most inclusive definition of a Protestant is one that stresses his repudiation of the authority of the see of Rome." [4] In the 1936 Census, non-Protestants are credited with 25,000,000 church members, of whom almost 20,000,000 were Roman Catholics. Simple subtraction of total church affiliation from the total population of the United States gives the number of "unchurched" Americans, the appalling figure of 70,000,000.

Since the religious groups outside Catholicism and Protestantism, defined in this wide sense, comprise less than 10 percent of the total church membership, and a still smaller proportion of the entire population of the United States, generalizations on the history of religion in America may, with some justification, ignore such denominations. But if generalizations are to interpret American church history, and not merely Protestant church history, they cannot ignore either the Roman Catholic Church or the great mass of the "unchurched."

The opposing systems of Catholicism and Protestantism started on most unequal footing in the history of the United States. When the new nation was constituted in the

---

[4] Silcox, Claris E. and Fisher, Galen M., *Catholics, Jews and Protestants,* p. 23. A discussion of the term "Protestant" will be found in the place cited.

closing years of the 18th Century, the few American Catholics were almost indiscernible among the Protestant multitudes. While the Federal Constitution guaranteed religious
freedom in its Bill of Rights, a number of the State Constitutions continued the establishment of Protestant
churches; and in those and in other States, laws inimical
to Catholicism were in force. Complete religious freedom
was not attained by Catholicism till well on in the 19th
Century.

Even when both religious systems had equal standing
before the law, the position of Protestantism was better
than that of Catholicism. The tradition of the country was
bitterly anti-Catholic. The power of wealth, influence and
political office was firmly in Protestant hands. The natural
increase of American Protestants and the influx of large
numbers of Protestant immigrants, particularly during the
Old Immigration, presaged a continuing Protestant domination of the American people.

Yet such domination has not been maintained.

Concomitantly with the development of Protestantism
in this country came the surge of two movements of the
greatest importance, the rapid expansion of American
Catholicism and the tremendous growth of infidelity.

Immigration has apparently been the greatest single
factor in the growth of the Catholic Church in the United
States. While in 1820 there were but 195,000 Catholics
among the 9,638,000 inhabitants of the United States,[5] a
century later Catholics numbered about 20,000,000 in a

[5] Guilday, Peter K., *John England*, I, p. 7.

population slightly above the 100,000,000 mark.[6] Immigration explains the increase, impressive both relatively and absolutely. While of the 33,654,803 immigrants who landed on our shores during the century in question, 19,062,190 came from countries predominantly non-Catholic (and their effect on present Protestant church statistics deserves study), 14,592,613 emigrated from nations that may be classified as Catholic.[7] The Catholic Church in the United States has been eminently successful in preserving the allegiance of these Catholic immigrants and their progeny, so successful that it has been and continues to be assailed as an "un-American," a "foreign" Church. Yet it should be a source of congratulation to sincere Christians that the Catholic Church has not been so narrowly "American" as to surrender millions of these new Americans to infidelity.

While indifferentism and other factors have continually drained off members from both Catholicism and Protestantism, the huge growth of infidelity has been accomplished in the last three generations. An eminent historian writes that, "Probably it would not be far out of the way to set down three-quarters of the inhabitants of the United States as belonging to some Christian organization in 1850, or at all events as considering themselves within the Chris-

---

[6] Garrison, Winfred E., *The March of Faith,* p. 197. Shaughnessy, Gerald, *Has the Immigrant Kept the Faith?,* p. 211.

[7] Shaughnessy, *op. cit.,* p. 244. These figures, of course, must be used with the greatest caution. For most of the century in question, statistics for re-migration to Europe were not compiled; large numbers of Protestants and other non-Catholics came from the countries listed as Catholic; possibly even larger numbers of Catholics came from the non-Catholic lands.

tian fold." [8] Since that time, however, the rural masses have, to a large extent, deserted the churches, and the churches, to an even larger extent, have abandoned the urban masses. Though each new publication of church statistics indicates an increased membership for practically all denominations (save the notable exceptions in the United States Religious Census for 1936), it is, to say the least, doubtful whether church attendance has kept up with church affiliation, and it is not at all doubtful that church statistics are notoriously unreliable. Certainly the mere existence of 70,000,000 Americans who do not maintain even a nominal connection with organized Christianity is sufficient proof that the churches have failed to retain the allegiance of large sections of the American people.

While the interaction of Protestantism and the American environment furnishes a most important aspect of the history of Christianity in the United States, other viewpoints must not be overlooked.

Why is the majority of Americans no longer Christian? The infidels of today were Christians but yesterday. The mere presence of the "unchurched," therefore, indicates weakness in Christianity, either Catholic or Protestant or both. Have both systems suffered losses proportionate to their numbers? Has either system shown itself better fitted to hold the allegiance of its members under conditions obtaining in this country and this age?

Why has the Catholic Church attained in America the preeminent position it now holds? Could it have acquired

[8] Channing, Edward, *History of the United States*, V, p. 220.

such strength if it were unsuited to American conditions, if it were not as truly American as it is truly Catholic?

A study of the general history of Christianity in the United States may supply sufficient data to suggest answers to these questions. It will be seen that the history of religion in this country is largely the story of the reactions of Catholicism and Protestantism to a frontier environment, whether that frontier has been the agricultural borderland treated at length by historians, or the industrial frontier offered to the churches by bourgeois and proletarian masses in the great American cities.

The history of our country has been illumined by great men and women, the character of whose lives may best be summed up by that jejune adjective "Christian." In a brief survey it would be impossible adequately to depict the effect of the truths common to both religious systems on these leaders or on the innumerable Americans whose lives have borne witness to the validity of those doctrines. While such a picture might be essential in a history of religion, it need not be attempted in a work whose narrower scope is to outline the institutional development of the Christian churches. The present work attempts to supply in a comprehensible form the essential facts of the historical evolution of those churches in the United States.

NOTE ON ECCLESIASTICAL STATISTICS

STATISTICS of church membership must be viewed with caution, since they are usually estimates, rather than the tabulations of censuses. Hall expresses a rather common opinion when he declares that "From the personal experience of the writer with church statistics, he would be inclined to take at least 15 to 20 percent off. The temptation for the individual church to exaggerate its numbers for the higher courts and assemblies is overwhelming and seldom resisted." [9]

The most commonly cited statistics of church membership are the estimates of the United States Religious Census. Since the method used is the rather crude one of accepting the estimates of each individual congregation, this government census is scarcely reliable, and its value very limited. It does present, however, the claims of the various denominations. Further, if a sect admits a notable loss of membership between censuses, such an admission—considering the laws of psychology—may be accepted as indicative of a trend. When the figures of the United States Religious Census are used in the text, these limitations have been considered.[10]

Another useful source of statistics is the *Year Book of*

[9] Hall, Thomas C., *Religious Background of American Culture*, p. 213.

[10] For the limitations of this census, cf. the official publication *Religious Bodies: 1916*, I, p. 13 ff. For an interesting analysis of the United States Religious Census of 1926, cf. Fry, Charles L., *The U. S. Looks at its Churches*. The author (p. vi) apparently overestimates the accuracy of the church membership statistics.

American Churches, published biennially under the auspices of the Federal Council of Churches. Inasmuch as the membership figures found in these volumes are the estimates not of the individual congregations but of the national headquarters of each church, they may be considered less credible than the statistics of the United States Religious Census.

Statistics of Catholic church membership are published in the annual *Official Catholic Directory.* Figures for three recent years may show the unreliability of these estimates. For the years 1939, 1940 and 1941, the *Directory* claims, respectively, 21,406,507, 21,403,136 and 22,293,101 Catholics. That a church which in one year lost 3,000 members could gain in the following year 890,000 new adherents is simply beyond the bounds of credibility. It has further been asserted that the estimates of the *Directory,* in contradistinction to the general run of church statistics, are too low rather than too high.[11]

The estimates of Catholic numbers found in the text are based chiefly on Bishop Gerald Shaughnessy's volume *Has the Immigrant Kept the Faith?* since his book is the outstanding scientific study of the problem and his results have, in the main, been accepted by scholars, both Catholic and non-Catholic. Reference has also been made to the estimates of Channing, Sweet, Bates, Guilday and others.

---

[11] Shaughnessy, *op. cit.,* p. 200 ff.

MAJOR TRENDS IN
AMERICAN CHURCH HISTORY

CHAPTER I

ORIGINS AND TYPES OF PROTESTANTISM

SINCE Catholicism and Protestantism are importations from Europe, some knowledge of the history of Christianity in the Old World is essential for a proper appreciation of the story of the Christian religions in the United States.[1] That history cannot be adequately treated in a brief chapter; only the broad outlines of the story can be drawn.

For a millennium before the discovery of America, there had existed in Europe a unity known as Christendom; and the bond of that unity was the Catholic Church. At one time the sway of Christendom had extended also over the Asiatic and African lands of the Mediterranean basin. By the end of the 7th Century, however, Islam dominated North Africa and districts of the Near East. In the 11th Century Eastern Christendom, under the leadership of the Patriarch of Constantinople, broke away from the Papacy and established the Eastern Orthodox Church. In Western Europe, however, the Catholic Church still preserved its preeminent position.

---

[1] It can be questioned whether the only two really indigenous American sects—the polytheistically-inclined Mormons, and the pantheistically-minded Christian Scientists—are Christian. Cf. Neve, J. L., *Churches and Sects of Christendom*, ch. XIV. Though the first American Baptist church originated here, its ideas were imported.

That preeminence did not remain unchallenged. Period-ically, heretical movements had disturbed the Church, cor-ruption in high places had undermined its authority, and centrifugal forces had strained its cohesive powers. Yet, during the course of that thousand years, none of these factors succeeded in shattering the religious unity of Western Europe. After every new attack, a purified Church had ultimately reestablished its dominion.

Twenty-five years after Columbus' great discovery, the unity of Christendom suffered a new assault. Forces not operative in former conflicts now were felt, and this latest onslaught succeeded in destroying the former religious unity. Under the pretense of a reformation of the Catholic Church, the movement, political and economic rather than religious, detached from the Church large sections of northern and western Europe.[2]

The political factor in the Protestant Revolt was supplied by the new cult of nationalism. The emergent national states were veering away from the ideal of a politically and religiously united Christendom. National monarchs were establishing despotisms which could be complete only with

[2] Baudrillart, Alfred, *The Catholic Church, the Renaissance and Protes-tantism*, p. 82: "Dollinger, Jannsen, and more recently Evers, have shown that it (the Protestant Revolt) was the consequence of a political and national rather than of a religious movement."

Vedder, Henry C., *The Reformation in Germany*, xlviii: "This was the real cause of the revolt from the Papacy that we call the Reformation (*sic*)—an economic and political struggle at bottom, to which the re-ligious aspect given by the initial quarrel about indulgences was merely incidental."

Latourette, Kenneth S., *History of the Expansion of Christianity*, IV, p. 33: "At its outset and for generations, Protestantism had sometimes been even more a political and a nationalistic than a religious movement."

regal control of subservient state churches. Kings, nobles and the new national patriots cast envious and covetous eyes on the Catholic Church. They desired to capture its prestige and convert its influence to their own ends.

Accusations of greed, leveled against the higher clergy of the Church, was one of the chief weapons of Protestant propagandists. Ironically enough, the avarice of Protestant leaders furnished the economic cause of the rupture of religious unity. The new middle-class capitalists, as well as the ruling aristocracy, coveted the Church's property, were restive under Church laws forbidding usury, and were rebellious against the Church's taxes and fees.[3]

The political and economic factors were not the sole causes of the Protestant Revolt; but they were its decisive elements. For the aristocracy and the bourgeoisie, alert for a pretext favorable to their own selfish ends, found and seized one in the complaints critical clerics, humanistic scholars, and the overburdened lower classes were bringing against abuses in the Church. Under the guidance of the upper classes, a movement for Church reform was turned into a religious revolt.

The Catholic Church reacted strongly to the challenge of the Protestant Revolt. An ecumenical council was convoked; at Trent the Church reaffirmed her doctrine and strengthened and purified her discipline. While the older Religious Orders were revivified, new congregations of

---

[3] Browne, Lewis, *Since Calvary*, p. 269: "The rulers were motivated undisguisedly by self interest. . . . (They) turned upon the hierarchical Church not because they felt morally outraged by its corruption, but because they were covetous of its wealth and power . . . With (the bourgeoisie), too, one of the motives for rebellion was self interest."

Religious were organized, and supplied the spearhead for the counter-attack on the new heresies. Southern Europe was kept intact within the body of Catholicism; large sections of western and northern Europe which earlier had succumbed to Protestantism were recovered. The Church's vitality was such that, coincidentally with reform and struggles against religious rebellion in Europe, she inaugurated and prosecuted in new lands across the seas one of the greatest missionary campaigns of all time.[4]

To recount the long, bitter and bloody story of the Protestant Revolt and the Catholic Reformation would be lengthy for this book. It must suffice here to note that the struggle subsided with Europe divided into two hostile religious systems.

While the long conflict was raging, the Protestant rebels perforce devised new systems of theology to supplant the teachings of the Catholic Faith. The new theologies took over bodily the great dogmas of the Catholic Church; and while divergencies were marked, all agreed on some peculiarly Protestant doctrines. The one immutable Protestant dogma was, and continues to be, the rejection of the Papacy.[5] Today members of all the major sects question or deny the divine inspiration of the Bible, but all early

---

[4] It must be understood that the Catholic Reformation was not a mere reaction to the Protestant Revolt. The Revolt itself was based on a movement for reform. For other and earlier attempts at reform, cf. Gasquet, Francis, *The Eve of the Reformation*, 5 ff.; Jourdan, George V., *The Movement toward Catholic Reform, passim;* Jannsen, Johann, *History of the German People,* I, *passim;* Pastor, Ludwig von, *History of the Popes,* V, p. 173 ff. On this Catholic missionary campaign, cf. Latourette, *op. cit.,* III.

[5] Silcox and Fisher, *op. cit.,* p. 32.

Protestants accepted Holy Writ as the inspired Word of God and as the sole source of revelation.[6] By their doctrine of private interpretation, the new sects made every man infallible, every man his own Pope; they wrecked the Catholic sacramental system, by rejecting all Sacraments except Baptism and the "Lord's Supper," and by giving to these two new and strange meanings.[7]

Early in the history of Protestantism, the heresiarchs saw that their system led to anarchy. Though in theory maintaining their dogma of private interpretation, they rejected it in practise. For they drew up and imposed on their followers scores of "creeds" and "confessions." All who openly denied the accepted Protestant teachings were considered heretics, and occasionally were treated as such. Calvin, for example, burned Servetus at the stake for "heresy"; Melanchthon, Luther's chief assistant, praised that execution as "a pious and memorable example for all posterity." [8]

On the basis of fundamental tendencies, Protestantism may be divided into four major categories, all of which played a part in the history of Christianity in the United States.

Lutheranism, the first of the new sects to emerge, seems to have had the least apparent effect on American Protestantism and on the religious history of the United States. With the acquiescence of its initiator, it early became, as

[6] Cavert, Samuel M. and H. P. Van Dusen, *Church Through Half a Century*, p. 163 ff.

[7] For the chaos in modern Protestant teaching on these two sacraments, cf. Dunkerly, Roderic and Arthur Headlam, *The Ministry and the Sacraments, passim.*

[8] Grisar, Hartmann, *Martin Luther*, p. 503.

did all Protestant denominations, a class sect.[9] Though many Germans and practically all Scandinavians eventually accepted the Lutheran creed, European Lutheranism became and remained the church of the Nordic upper classes.

In America, only the synodical type has been adopted, but European Lutheran polity assumed either episcopal or synodal form. Lutheran bishops, however, are considered merely administrative officials, not priests of a higher rank. The new Lutheran faith received its most important credal expression in the "Augsburg Confession." Its most singular doctrine was, and continues to be, the dogma of justification by faith alone, with the consequent rejection of good works as a means to salvation.[10] While Luther condoned bigamy and other questionable practices, Lutheranism adopted the moral code of the Catholic Church without major change.[11] Lutheran worship was "cleansed" of the Mass and of the other ritual ceremonies of the Catholic Church; the pulpit assumed the place once occupied by the altar.

The second of the major Protestant categories, initiated by the dour John Calvin, enrolled adherents chiefly in

[9] Niebuhr, H. Richard, *Social Sources of Denominationalism,* p. 6: "Denominations represent the accommodation of religion to the caste system . . ." Bates, Ernest S., *American Faith,* p. 50: "Luther knew that his own safety depended upon his aristocratic following . . . For a time he strove to steer a middle course, but when the crisis became acute, he definitely joined the party of wealth and authority."

[10] Hall, *op. cit.,* p. 276. *Concordia Cyclopaedia, sub voce* "Justification," p. 381: "Our works have no place whatever in our justification, neither as a cause nor as a means."

[11] Grisar, *op. cit.,* p. 513 ff.; Clayton, Joseph, *Luther and His Work,* p. 173 ff. For an interesting apology of Luther's stand on bigamy, cf. Boehmer, Heinrich, *Luther and the Reformation,* p. 213 ff.

Switzerland, the Low Countries, and Scotland.[12] Early Calvinism found its main support among the bourgeoisie; this caste appeal of Calvinism still persists. "Calvinism remains the religion of a middle class which excludes from its worship, by the character of its appeal, the religious poor as well as those who live within the lower ranges of economic and cultural respectability." [13] The joint rise of Calvinism and capitalism is a phenomenon which has led some students to see in Calvin's religion a most important causal relationship to the growth of capitalism.[14]

The polity of Calvinism is synodical. Its credal expression most important for American religious history is the "Westminster Confession." The chief doctrines of Calvinism are unconditional predestination, the total depravity of man, the particular atonement, irresistible grace, and final perseverance. The most notorious of these doctrines is that of predestination, which taught that all men save the "elect" were doomed to hell from all eternity, irrespective of their acts in this life. This inhuman doctrine was buttressed by the dogma that every action of man, even

[12] Bates, *op. cit.,* p. 66: "When all is said on his behalf that can be said, he (Calvin) remains the outstanding example among Protestants of the way in which religious fanaticism can change men into monsters."

[13] Niebuhr, *op. cit.,* p. 105.

[14] A whole literature on the question has been published. Cf. *inter alios,* Weber, Max, *Protestant Ethic and the Spirit of Capitalism;* Tawney, R. H., *Religion and the Rise of Capitalism;* Fanfani, Amintore, *Catholicism, Protestantism and Capitalism.*

Members of the Calvinistic denominations did not resent the flattering impeachment until the Great Depression of 1929 tarnished the shining repute of the capitalistic system. Then capitalism was discovered to be a diabolical machination of the Jesuits. Cf. Brodrick, James, *The Economic Morals of the Jesuits.*

his prayer to God, was a sin, so thoroughly was man depraved by the fall of Adam. Logically connected with these beliefs were the Calvinistic dogmas that Christ died to atone, not for the sins of all men, but merely for the faults of the elect; that His grace, which cannot be rejected by man, is given only to the predestined; and that, consequently, the elect cannot, even if they would, escape their happy lot.

Early Calvinism imposed on its adherents, together with these chilling dogmas, a worship void of all rites or liturgy, and a pharisaic code of behavior. The way of life, for example, of the early New England Calvinists had made the term "Puritan" notorious.

It would indeed be strange if such a religion did not produce a strong reaction. Arminianism, named after one of its early leaders, the Dutch pastor Jacob Hermanzoon, arose within Calvinism as a protest against its insupportable creed. This milder theological school taught a conditional predestination, based on man's merits; universal atonement; a doctrine of "free grace," given freely to all men and freely accepted or rejected by them; and the need for man's cooperation in salvation.

Though Arminianism was adjudged heretical by early synods, gradually it permeated all save the most rigidly Calvinistic sects. It was a forerunner of the later "liberal" Protestant thought which has brought about the complete rejection of the Calvinistic theology.

The third of the great divisions of Protestantism is Anglicanism. Its origin in the lusts of Henry VIII of England is too well known to need emphasis.[15] Considering its founder and the class which profited by the confiscation of Catholic Church property in England, not unexpectedly the new Anglican church was a sect of the upper classes. Its polity is episcopal. Originally Catholic, but with the King assuming the place of the Pope, it passed from schism to heresy under the influence of Continental Protestantism. Its chief credal expression is contained in the Thirty Nine Articles, which, though reared on a Lutheran foundation, are capable of a Calvinistic, an Arminian, and even of a Catholic interpretation. Anglicanism was and remains the most ritualistic of the Protestant sects.

The fourth major category of Protestantism arose among the lower economic classes. In the earliest days of the Protestant Revolt, the poor and the uneducated found themselves cheated by the new churches. Only the middle and upper classes profited by the establishment of the new denominations; the lower classes were left to shift for themselves.[16] Since the aristocracy and the bourgeoisie saw to it that the poor did not return to the Catholic Church, many proletarians, particularly among the English and Germans,

[15] Bates, *op. cit.,* p. 60: "No other Protestant church ever had so simple or so discreditable an origin."

[16] *Ibid,* p. 34: "In many ways, they (Calvin and Luther) represented a betrayal of the Reformation (*sic*). . . . The Reformation began as a radical lower-class movement which was largely taken over by the rising bourgeoisie under Luther and Calvin, to be followed by a renewed struggle between these two classes within Protestantism itself." Niebuhr, *op. cit.,* p. 34: "The Protestant Revolt failed to satisfy the lower classes after taking Catholicism away. The new Protestant churches were middle-class and aristocratic. . . . The failure of the Reformation to meet the religious needs of the peasants and other disfranchised groups is a chapter writ large in history."

expressed their religious needs and aspirations in a novel type of religion known as Evangelicalism.

Evangelicalism is of supreme importance in the history of Protestantism in the United States. The typical American sect is Evangelical; the largest, the most important and the least stable American denominations are found in this category.[17]

Though the innumerable Evangelical sects have assumed many forms and names, and though they have manifested manifold idiosyncrasies of teaching and worship, all these sects of the disinherited have some significant characteristics in common and follow a typical evolutionary pattern.

In the origin of a typical Evangelical sect, the poor and the uneducated found the established sect unsuited to their needs, and so tended to form within it congregations composed exclusively of lower-class members. Gradually these congregations of the disinherited drew apart from the parent denomination, established fraternal relations with other groups experiencing a similar process of evolution, broke relations with the parent sect, and established an independent denomination. Almost invariably, the polity of the new sect was congregational;[18] its worship, moral

[17] Rowe, *op. cit.*, p. 158: "The largest number of religious people (in the U.S.) were Protestants, and belonged to churches that made an emotional experience basic in religion. 'Conversion' was the technical term in use to explain that experience. . . ."

[18] Congregational polity is one of the great marks of Evangelicalism. The Methodist Episcopalians are a singular exception to this general rule among the larger sects. This exception is explained by the fact that, although the early membership of the Methodist church was almost exclusively lower class, the sect founders were members of the middle class.

teachings, and doctrinal tenets assumed a form conditioned always by the poverty and ignorance of its adherents.

While such a new sect manifested the theological proclivities of its parent denomination, whether Calvinistic or Arminian, Lutheran or Anglican, it invariably based its theology on the peculiar Evangelical doctrine of "conversion." This dogma taught that man was "saved," not by the justification of faith or by the predestination of God alone, but by an emotional upheaval through which sinful man is "convinced of sin," and "accepts the Lord." Apparently the ignorance of the disinherited, which permitted them to confuse religion with emotionalism, and the economic disabilities, which forced them to seek emotional catharsis in their worship rather than in costly recreation, were important factors in the universal adoption of this peculiar doctrine by the Evangelicals.

Fundamental to the "conversion" was a belief that the Holy Spirit acted directly on man's emotions. Since only adults could experience the "conversion," sects of Calvinistic antecedents were forced logically to accept the inhuman doctrine that all who died before attaining the use of reason were condemned to hell. Opposition to this cruel dogma of "infant damnation" was a factor in the later liberalizing of Protestant theology. Some Evangelical sects believed that a second emotional upheaval "sanctified" a man who had already been "justified." In some of these sects, antinomianism resulted. Those who professed to have received this "Second Blessing" considered themselves "perfect," incapable of sin. The consequences of such an aberration are evident. The "perfect," "confirmed in grace," deliberately performed acts in contravention of all morality; they considered these deeds licit, and rejected remorse of conscience as a temptation of the devil.

Another doctrine typical of Evangelicalism was millennarianism. Affirmation of the imminence of Christ's Second Coming, when the poor will inherit the earth, was readily made under the influence of the economic conditions of the sect membership, and was bound to be reflected in the sect theology.

Evangelical denominations stressed emotionalism not only in their theology, but also in their worship. Their divine services were marked by devices calculated to stir up strong feelings. Highly emotional hymns were sung; vividly colored sermons were preached; groans, sobs, shouts and other expressions of emotionalism were encouraged in their congregations. If, because of overwrought nerves, an unfortunate became hysterical, unconscious, or unintelligible in speech, the deluded sect members believed that the Holy Spirit had descended upon the poor sufferer.[19]

The preaching of a Puritan way of life was another distinctive mark of the new Evangelical sect. This was but another reflection of the poverty of the sect members. Rich dress, liquor, dancing, theater-going, and other "worldly" amusements beyond the economic reach of the sect membership were condemned as "sinful."

The Evangelical sects have proven more susceptible to change than the other categories of Protestantism. Evangelical mutations follow a classical evolutionary pattern.

[19] Even today some Evangelical sects encourage emotionalism of this type. For examples, cf. Clark, Elmer T., Small Sects in America, ch. IV.

Over a period of years the membership of the new sect, partly because of emphasis on Puritan morality and thrift, gains in wealth and acquires a degree of respectability. Imperceptibly the sect becomes tinged with a bourgeois mentality, and is somewhat shamefaced about its antecedents.[20] If the doctrine of millennarianism and the "Second Blessing" had been taught, they are now tacitly and tactfully forgotten. Since the new respectability views sensationalism with disfavor, emotionalism in the "conversion" and in worship are gradually eliminated. The Puritanical code of behavior is progressively abandoned. The matter has been put rather cynically: "Those pinched by economic circumstances look askance at theater-going, card-playing, and 'putting on of gold and costly' apparel, but indulge in the same when their earthly fortunes improve." [21] The sect becomes, in all but name, indistinguishable from a dozen other bourgeois denominations.

Often has it happened that sect members who had lagged behind in the acquisition of wealth and respectability find the denomination, in its final stages of evolution, no longer capable of satisfying their peculiar religious needs. Once more, therefore, Evangelicalism begins the evolution of a new sect. These poor and uneducated folk tend to draw apart in congregations of their own; and the groundwork of a new denomination has been laid. Niebuhr sums up the process: ". . . . One phase of the history of denominationalism reveals itself as the story of the religiously neg-

[20] Niebuhr, *op. cit.,* p. 54: "The churches of the poor all become middle-class churches sooner or later. . . ."

[21] Clark, *op. cit.,* p. 19. Cf. Mecklin, John M., *The Story of American Dissent,* p. 26.

lected poor, who fashion a new type of Christianity which corresponds to their distinctive needs, who rise in the economic scale under the influence of religious discipline, and who, in the midst of a freshly acquired cultural respectability, neglect the new poor succeeding them on a lower plane. This pattern occurs with remarkable regularity in the history of Christianity. Anabaptists, Quakers, Methodists, the Salvation Army, and more recent sects of like type illustrate this rise and progress of the churches of the disinherited." [22]

Protestant denominations may be conveniently classified as Lutheran or Calvinistic, Anglican or Evangelical. This is a workable rule, even though the strict category of some sects may be difficult to decide. To trace the origin of each sub-division within these categories would be an impossible task, for Protestantism has an embarrassing fecundity in the production of new sects. The adjective "fissiparous" has been adopted practically as a technical term to express this mark of the church. Notably in the United States, the analogy of "fissiparous" cell-division has been conspicuous in Protestantism. Causes apparently of the least moment have been sufficient to start a new sect on its career.[23] It would be impracticable to explore the origins of the more than 250 sects now extant in the United States, but since some explanation of their propagation is essential, a tabulation of their major causes is indicated.

1. Class divisions, as explained in the evolution of Evan-

[22] Niebuhr, *op. cit.,* p. 28. For a similar viewpoint, cf. Mecklin, *op. cit.,* p. 4 ff.
[23] For some of these causes of schism, cf. Carroll, H. K., *Religious Forces of the United States,* p. xxiii ff.

gelical sects, have been of frequent occurrence in our religious history. As the original lower-class Methodists separated from the Anglicans, so the Holiness sects broke away from the later middle-class Methodists.

2. Nationalism has produced a large group of denominations. American, German, Danish, Swedish, Norwegian, Finnish, Icelandic, and Slovak Lutherans all have their independent national synods in this country.

3. Debates over the language to be used in divine worship have occasioned new sects. The German Albright Methodists and some Lutheran groups are attributable to this cause.

4. Sectionalism has produced its sects. The Mason-Dixon Line divides northern Baptists and Presbyterians from the schismatic sects of the same denominations in the South.

5. Racism has caused an almost complete separation of colored from white Christians. Over 90 percent of all Negro Christians are enrolled in exclusively colored denominations.

6. Immigration has carried with it large numbers of new sects. In recent years, England alone has sent us Darbyites, Irvingites, and other small groups. Other immigrants found the branch of their sect, established in this country by previous immigrants, changed beyond recognition; therefore they founded their own sects. The Christian Reformed Church is an example of this type.

7. The problem of polity has partitioned sects. The Evangelical tendency towards a congregational polity has caused many schisms from the Methodists.

8. Administration of the "sacraments," particularly Bap-

tism, has caused friction within sects, and has resulted in their final fracture. The River Brethren, with their singular doctrine on the "sacrament" of foot-washing, broke into factions over its administration. One sect insisted that the same man should wash and dry the feet, the other that one man should wash, and another dry.

9. Quarrels over forms of worship have ended in schism. The "un-Scriptural" use of organs in church was a major cause of the separation of the Churches of Christ from the Disciples of Christ.

10. Disputed "moral" questions have broken sects asunder. The Mennonites have proven especially susceptible to fine distinctions in settling "moral" problems. New Mennonite sects have originated in disputes over the morality of top buggies, horse trades, even the cut of a minister's coat.

11. Opposition to such "un-Scriptural" novelties as Sunday Schools, missionary societies and an educated ministry has caused schisms, particularly among the Hard Shell or Landmarker Baptists.

12. Individual church leaders, moved by ambition or even less laudable motives, have led their personal following out of the established sect and have founded new denominations to their own taste. A number of Holiness sects have been established by such leaders.

13. Theological disputes have precipitated a number of schisms. The unity of churches has been destroyed by arguments on the relative merits of Calvinism versus Arminianism, Unitarianism versus Trinitarianism, Fundamentalism versus Modernism.

The interminable divisions within Protestantism are

openly lamented by leading Protestant churchmen. A widespread "ecumenical movement" has, in the past generation, been seeking the consolidation of Protestant denominations. Protestant spokesmen, however, continue to make a virtue of necessity, by defending the multitudinous schisms as "new impulses of the message of Jesus," as new manifestations of the "vitality of the Christian message." Latourette, for example, expresses a typical view: "Some (sects) were born of envy, strife and personal ambition, but of the larger ones the great majority sprang primarily from fresh expressions of the Christian impulse. In Protestantism they corresponded roughly to the new orders and congregations in the Roman Catholic Church." [24] While such wishful thinking may enhearten Protestant churchmen, such comparisons are without foundation in reality; for Catholic Religious Orders strengthen rather than destroy the unity of the Mystical Body of Christ which is His Church. In Catholic eyes, the multitudinous sects and schisms of Protestantism give but a further proof that the one true Church of Christ is not to be found within Protestantism.

[24] Latourette, *op. cit.*, IV, p. 41.

CHAPTER II

THE COLONIAL BACKGROUND: SPANISH AND FRENCH MISSIONS

THE history of the United States, as well as the history of the Christian religions in the Western Hemisphere, opens with the story of Catholic missionary endeavors.

The chronicles of these early Catholic missionaries is, unfortunately, a closed book to most Americans. Historians, it is true, laud the labors of the early Padres, and point out the significance of their work. MacLeod, for example, declares: "No enterprise in the world's history was ever more vast in its ambitions; and none so vast was ever carried on against larger odds, or with more intelligence, heroism and energy." [1] Bolton, speaking of but one of the many missionary Orders engaged in the field, writes: "No phase of western hemisphere history reveals greater heroism, and few have greater significance than that of the Jesuit missions." [2]

Due in great measure to the influence of Parkman's famous volume on the French Black Robes, some small information on the French missionary endeavor has found its way into the average American text-book. But the

[1] MacLeod, William C., *The American Indian Frontier*, pp. 103-104.
[2] Bolton, Herbert E., *Rim of Christendom*, p. 3.

Spanish missions were far more important. As Bolton writes: "The Black Robes of New France counted their conversions by hundreds, or at best by thousands; those of New Spain, working in a more propitious vineyard, numbered their baptisms by hundreds of thousands, or even by millions." [3] The facts about the Spanish Padres are very generally ignored; the concept of the average American about their labors is derived from the distorted fables of the infamous "Black Legend." Many generations of American schoolboys have been exposed to this unhistorical tale of Spanish and Portuguese Catholic colonial ineptitude, faithlessness, cruelty, greed and bigotry.[4] Forty years ago, Bourne noted: "To the prolonged efforts of the (Spanish) Crown in behalf of its Indian vassals many a popular history gives less space than to the terrible stories of cruelties which Las Casas heaped up." [5] His judgment could be justly applied to many more recent books.

The tale of Spanish and Portuguese Catholicism in colonial America is one certain to stir not revulsion but admiration. Since the labors of the Portuguese missionaries in Brazil have not influenced the course of Catholicism in the United States, their interesting story finds no place in this narrative. Necessarily, however, the chronicle of the Spanish missionary priests who toiled within the present boundaries of the United States must be prefaced by a brief overview of Catholic missions in colonial Spanish America. Catholicism in Latin America has an early history which

[3] *Ibid*, p. 4.

[4] A report of the American Council on Education declared that in 1944 this "Black Legend" still had "widespread perpetuation" in text-books.

[5] Bourne, Edward G., *Spain in America*, p. 253.

suggests interesting comparisons and contrasts with Protestantism in colonial English America, particularly in two important aspects of the history of religion in the western hemisphere, the philosophy of each religious system governing its relations with the aborigines and the reactions of either system to the presence of the Negroes, both slave and free.

It has been noted that the period from the discovery of America to the American Revolution was one of the greatest missionary epochs in the history of the Roman Catholic Church. As Spain, Portugal and France expanded overseas, the Church grew with them and beyond them. When the force of the early missionary impulse had waned, the new mission fields in Asia, Africa and the two Americas numbered the new accretions to the Church by the millions.

The most brilliant achievement of this great expansion was undoubtedly the work of the Church in Spanish America. When the first ominous rumblings of the Protestant Revolt were perceived in Europe, the Church had completed a score of years of labor in the New World. For missionary activity had begun with the second voyage of Columbus to the lands he had discovered.

The American missions were generally staffed by members of the Religious Orders. Large numbers of Franciscans, Dominicans, Augustinians, Jesuits and other Religious made the perilous voyage to the new lands, and scattered throughout the length and breadth of Spanish America. In many instances these zealous priests were not content merely to follow the Spanish flag; again and again, eager missionaries penetrated into unexplored territories with the

Conquistadors or before them. Many paid for their daring
by death at the hands of the Indians; many others succumbed to fatigue and disease. Yet their work prospered
marvelously.

With amazing rapidity, and in even more amazing numbers, the Indians became Catholics. Almost incredible records of mass conversions are chronicled. It is reported, for
example, that the Franciscan Peter of Ghent, with the assistance of but a single colleague, baptized 200,000 of the
aborigines.[6] The actual number of the converts to Catholicism will never be known. Yet while estimates vary greatly,
all agree that the total was immense. MacLeod, speaking
only of the Spanish cities and towns, estimates that they
contained, after but seventy-five years of missionary activity,
about 5,000,000 Catholic Indians.[7] Mexico alone, within a
few years of the landing of Cortez, had contributed millions of new members to the Church. Latourette cites a
report of Mexican Catholics in the year 1536, and declares:
"Even the extreme total of 10,500,000 appears possible."[8]
Whatever the actual number of Christian Indians may have
been, this fact is certain: by the time of the first English
settlement in the North American mainland, large portions
of Spanish America were Catholic.

The history of colonial Spanish America is not without
its dark pages. There, as in all new colonies, exploitation
of the aborigines early assumed serious proportions. The
Catholic Church, however, reacted quickly and vigorously

[6] Latourette, *op. cit.*, V, p. 113.
[7] MacLeod, William C., "Contacts of Europe with the American
Aborigines," in *European Civilization*, VII, p. 901.
[8] Latourette, *op. cit.*, V, p. 113.

against the oppression of the Indians. The missionaries, notably the saintly Bartolome de Las Casas, the Dominican bishop who is one of the greatest figures in the history of the American frontier, carried on at the Spanish and Papal Courts a continued and effective propaganda in defense of the savages. Under the influence of Catholicism the Spanish Crown enacted a series of most enlightened laws, admired today for their humaneness, designed to protect the liberty and property of the savage subjects of Spain. The Papacy, reinforcing temporal penalties with spiritual punishment, decreed the excommunication of any who enslaved the Indians. In many instances Spanish colonists flaunted the laws of both Church and State. Yet within a century of the discovery of America, the practise of Indian slavery had been destroyed. MacLeod asserts: "Enslavement of the Indians in Latin America never became of prime importance in the history of the Indian because of the influences brought to bear against the practise of enslavement by Pope, King and monk." [9]

Whatever charges of cruelty to the aborgines may be brought against individual Spaniards, the record of New Spain vis-a-vis the Indians is truly admirable, especially in contrast to that of British colonial America. For through the influence of Catholicism, the Indians of Spanish America were not only saved from the virtual extinction meted out to their northern brethren at the hands of the English, but were brought within the ambitus of Spanish civilization and made partakers of Spanish culture.

The Church performed a similar work for the Negroes,

[9] MacLeod, *American Indian Frontier*, p. 299.

who, as in British colonial America, formed a large portion of the population. The Negroes appeared in both Spanish and British America as slaves. And, as slaves everywhere, their defenseless state provided an unresisting means of exploitation. In Latin America, however, the efforts of Catholicism to ameliorate the lot of the slaves were continuous and effective. Under the pressure of priestly propaganda, laws were enacted which restricted the powers of masters over their slaves, mitigated harsh conditions of labor, and guaranteed to the slave the right of legal redress against his master. As Bourne asserts: "A comparative study of the status and treatment of slaves in the Spanish, French and English colonies reveals the fact, surprising today, so widespread is the view that the Spanish colonial system was pre-eminently oppressive, that the Spanish slave code was far more humane than either the French or English slave laws." [10]

Nor was the influence of Catholicism used merely to protect the slaves. The first man in the New World to raise his voice in protest against slavery and the slave trade was the Jesuit priest, Alfonso Sandoval. His protest was seconded by ever increasing numbers of the clergy. The effectiveness of this propaganda may be gauged by the fact that, a century before the American Civil War, the majority of Negroes in many parts of Spanish America were free men.[11] Due largely to the Catholic Church, the universal emancipation of the Negro in Spanish America

---

[10] Bourne, *op. cit.,* p. 280. For these laws, cf. Bourne, *loc. cit.,* and Latourette, *op. cit.,* IV, p. 98.

[11] Bourne, *op. cit.,* p. 281.

was accomplished without the effusion of blood; and generally speaking the liberation of the slaves was completed
before 1860.

Yet Catholic efforts for the welfare and manumission of
the Negro slaves were but secondary objectives of the
Church. The primary end was always the Christianization
of the colored people. Many priests devoted their lives to
the service of the Negroes. The incredibly mortified life,
for example, of the Jesuit Saint, Peter Claver, accomplished
marvelous results. It is estimated that he alone baptized
300,000 Negro neophytes. While some Indian tribes, hidden
in remote jungle or mountain fastnesses, escaped the ministrations of the Catholic missionaries, the Negroes, always
located in or near Spanish settlements, came under the
daily influence of the Church. Parish priests, as part of
their regular parochial duties, taught the Negroes the
truths of the Catholic religion and attended to their
spiritual needs. The results of this continual apostolate were
striking. While the majority of slaves in British America
remained outside the pale of organized Protestantism, the
great majority of the Negroes in Spanish America em-
braced the Catholic religion. While emancipation in the
United States was immediately followed by a mass movement of Negro Christians into exclusively colored denominations, the free Negroes of Spanish America were content
to remain within the Church that had served them so long
and so well. A Negro scholar has summed up the contrasting reactions of Catholicism and Protestantism to the
Negro in America in these words. "It seems, then, in view
of these comparisons, that the religious freedom gained by

the Protestants in their revolt against the Catholic Church has too often turned out to be an additional license to hate the brother of color. While the Protestant slave-holders in the United States were writing and rewriting arguments to prove that the Negroes were brutes and therefore should be enslaved as beasts of burden, the Catholics were accepting the Negroes as brethren and treating them as men. Seeing in the slaves themselves great potentiality for the enjoyment of more culture and for contributions thereto, the Latins gave Negroes opportunities far greater than those which were found in Protestant America." [12]

While the work among the Indians and the Negroes in Spanish America engrossed the attention and the energies of the Catholic Church, the territories within the present boundaries of the United States were not neglected. The Spanish Padres were laboring to convert the Indians north of the Rio Grande two generations before the first English settler landed at Jamestown. Catholic priests began their labors within the boundaries of the original Thirteen States by the middle of the 16th Century. When the colony of Virginia, destined never to send a single missionary to the Indians, was founded, Spanish Franciscans and Jesuits were ministering to an estimated 10,000 Catholic Indians in Florida and Georgia. [13] These mission fields, which in their days of greatest development had served about 30,000 mission Indians, were utterly destroyed before 1740 by the growing British power. [14] A non-Catholic historian writes

[12] Woodson, Carter G., "Negro Slavery," *European Civilization*, VII, p. 591.

[13] MacLeod, "Contacts," p. 871.

[14] Latourette, *op. cit.*, III, p. 133.

of this deed: "Carolina's place in the history of Christian missions lies in her only achievement in this field—the utter destruction of the missions of Guale and Apalatchee in Georgia and Florida below, achieved with the aid of cannibal bands of savages, followed by the burning at the stake by the savage auxiliaries of three Franciscan Fathers, missionaries, and fourteen Christian Indians, and the enslavement of 1,400 other mission Indians." [15]

In territories later acquired by the American moulders of manifest destiny, the Catholic Church was at work when Virginia was only a dream. At the close of the 16th Century Franciscan friars penetrated the forbidding lands north of the Rio Grande and initiated the work of Christianization. By 1630 the missions situated in the present State of New Mexico ministered to an estimated 60,000 Indian Catholics.[16] An Indian revolt against Spanish rule in 1680 brought about the death of many friars and the destruction of the mission field. Within a few years, however, the Franciscans courageously returned and rebuilt the shattered structure of the mission. Until the anti-clerical government of newly independent Mexico crippled the work in the early 19th Century, the Indian Catholic population of New Mexico averaged in numbers between 10,000 and 15,000.[17] From bases in Mexico missionary excursions were made into sparsely populated Texas. Considering the few numbers of nomadic Indians and the great difficulties of

15 MacLeod, "Contacts," p. 887.

16 Latourette, *op. cit.*, III, p. 125. Cf. Scholes, France V., *Church and State in New Mexico: 1610-1650,* and *Troublous Times in New Mexico: 1659-1670,* for illustrative background material.

17 Latourette, *loc. cit.*

that inhospitable missionary field, the Texas mission stations enjoyed a remarkable measure of success.[18]

Successful, too, were the missions to the West. Pioneer work in Arizona and California was under the direction of the Jesuits, notably Eusebio Kino and Juan de Salvatierra.[19] When the Society of Jesus was expelled, shortly before the American Revolution, from all Spanish possessions, the Franciscans, under the leadership of the great missionary, Junipero Serra, assumed the burden of these western missions. At their peak, the California missions numbered about 50,000 Indian Catholics (*circa* 1800).[20] Before Upper California had been acquired by the United States, disease had greatly reduced the numbers of mission Indians, and government opposition had hampered the friars.

This brief survey of early Catholicism in the southern and southwestern sections of the present United States does but meager justice to the tremendous labors of the Spanish missionaries. In view of the history of colonial British America, the effect of this Catholicism is more strikingly illustrated by a purely negative norm. As Gorman points out, "This one glorious truth stands prominent: the Spaniards in the United States did not drive the natives from their homes or oppress them, much less destroy them. These accusations, if made at all, must fall on some other race." [21]

[18] Cf. Castaneda, Carlos E., *Our Catholic Heritage in Texas*, III, p. 110 ff. *et passim*.

[19] Bolton, *op. cit.*, pp. 6-25, gives a brief description of the Jesuit missionary activity on the United States-Mexican border.

[20] Latourette, *op. cit.*, III, p. 131.

[21] O'Gorman, Thomas, *History of the Roman Catholic Church in the United States*, p. 113.

Catholicism in New France has written an equally honorable and memorable record. Mission activity among the Canadian Indians began early in the 17th Century. As were the Spanish padres of the South and Southwest, the French missionaries were mostly Franciscans and Jesuits. The course of the missionary labors of the French priests was the course of French penetration of North America. The Black Robes advanced with the *couriers du bois* up the valley of the St. Lawrence, thence along the shores of the Great Lakes into the present territory of the United States.

The earliest labors of the Jesuits among the Algonquins of the St. Lawrence valley and the Huron tribes above Lake Erie were crowned with notable success. By 1640 Huronia, with a population of 20,000 aborigines, was "virtually a mission state." [22] This happy condition of affairs did not perdure. By mid-century the mission state had been destroyed by the Iroquois in their bitter war of extermination against the Algonquins and Hurons. Parkman writes: "The cause of the failure of the Jesuits is obvious. The guns and tomahawks of the Iroquois were the ruins of their hopes." [23] This statement, however, requires considerable modification. While a very large proportion of the Catholic Indians met death at the hands of the Five Tribes, sizeable remnants of the shattered Huron lodges escaped to territories less accessible to Iroquois warparties. These Indians, due to the perservering Black Robes

---

[22] MacLeod, *American Indian Frontier,* p. 118.
[23] Parkman, Francis, *The Jesuits in North America,* p. 551.

who journeyed with them, preserved their allegiance to their new religion.

The obnoxious obtrusion of the Iroquois drew the attention of the Jesuits to the Indians of that Confederation. As a consequence, several apparently unsuccessful endeavors to reduce the Five Tribes to Christianity were launched. The most renowned results of these missionary efforts were the martyrdom of St. Isaac Jogues and his companions and the conversion of Kateri Tekakwitha, the "Lily of the Mohawks."

The missions to the Iroquois, however, were anything but failures. Indeed, considering the extreme difficulties of that mission field, the labors of the Black Robes were eminently successful. The number of Iroquois Catholics was never impressive, because the numbers of the Iroquois were small. The continual wars of those bellicose tribes had reduced them from 30,000 in the middle of the 17th Century to but 7,000 a hundred years later.[24] Of this latter number at least a fifth were Catholics.[25] Before 1750 large groups of the Five Tribes had established themselves permanently in the Catholic Indian settlements of Canada— "the Cayugas (moved) almost bodily, and the Mohawks leaving not a soul behind."[26] The continued devotion to

[24] MacLeod, *American Indian Frontier*, p. 289.

[25] *Ibid*, p. 289: "The influence of the Jesuits drew off to a French mission . . . about one-fifth of the Iroquois population." It appears, however, that the proportion may have been larger. Hughes, Thomas, *History of the Society of Jesus in North America*, II (text), p. 414, finds that at the end of the Colonial Period about 900 Iroquois warriors and their families were in the Canadian Catholic missions, while less than 2,000 Iroquois braves, many of them adopted from tribes not members of the Iroquois Confederation, were left in English New York.

[26] Hughes, *op. cit.*, II (text), p. 381.

Catholicism of the descendants of these Iroquois furnishes but another proof that the labors of Jogues and his colleagues cannot be considered anything but a success. It was, indeed, far-wandering Iroquois who inspired the moving appeal of the Pacific Coast tribes in 1820 to the Jesuits in St. Louis for Black Robes to come and work among them.

French Jesuits were also found evangelizing the Indian tribes of Maine. In that territory the Black Robes went in peril of their lives, not so much at the tomahawks of the aborigines as at the guns of the English. The Massachusetts Puritans watched with jaundiced eye the increasing number of "Praying" Indians. Preferring Indians as dead pagans rather than live Catholics, they were particularly incensed by the successes of Father Sebastian Rale (or Rasle). The narrow Calvinists organized a military expedition to dispose of the Jesuits and to crush the power of their neophytes. In the campaign that followed, known as "Father Rale's War," the obnoxious missionary was killed and his corpse mutilated.[27] The mission field, however, was not abandoned. And in the Revolutionary War, the Praying Indians of Maine were among the few groups of redmen who aided the colonial cause.

The French missionary activity in the United States was not confined merely to the Eastern Seaboard States. The Black Robes ranged widely throughout the Old Northwest. Marquette labored in Michigan and, after his epochal voyage of discovery, established the first mission station in Illinois; Allouez, the "Apostle of the Northwest," evan-

[27] O'Gorman, *op. cit.*, p. 138 ff.; Hughes, *op. cit.*, II (text), p. 272 ff.

gelized the Indians of Michigan and Wisconsin. The shores of the Great Lakes were dotted with Jesuit mission stations, and Black Robes were to be found as far afield as the plains of the Dakotas, the forests of the Lake of the Woods, and the forbidding shores of Hudson's Bay. Other French Jesuits were at work in the South. From a base in New Orleans, eager missionaries pressed north along the Mississippi and its tributaries and evangelized the Indian tribes of Louisiana, Mississippi and Arkansas.[28]

This far-ranging missionary activity of the Black Robes was abruptly halted by the expulsion of the Society of Jesus from all French possessions near the close of the Colonial Period. But shortly after the new United States acquired Louisiana from Napoleon, the Black Robes returned to begin a new and continuing missionary activity among the Indians of the United States.

A brief summary of intense missionary activity extending throughout a quarter of a millennium is inevitably inadequate. Nevertheless, enough data has been supplied to indicate the marvelous achievements of the Catholic Church in colonial America. While our narrative has ignored the ordinary parochial work of the Church among the European colonists, that that humdrum task was eminently successful is indicated by the fact that today the words "French Canadian" and "Latin American" are practically synonymous with the term "Catholic." Through the perservering efforts of her missionaries, a continent and a half have been added to the widespread domains of the Church. On the groundwork laid by her apostolic priests, nuns and

[28] Delanglez, Jean, *French Jesuits in Lower Louisiana: 1700-1763.*

Brothers, the Church has erected an edifice in which millions of her children, black, white and red, worship on terms of equality as children of one common Father. The Catholic Church has ample reason to hold in veneration the memory of the zealous missionaries of New France and New Spain.

CHAPTER III

THE COLONIAL BACKGROUND: BRITISH AMERICA

A S THE average American concept of Spanish colonial history has been distorted by the "Black Legend," so some fables of our American folklore have for generations falsely colored the picture of British colonial history in the present United States.

Completely outside the legitimate scope of history was the belief that Divine Providence did not permit the penetration of the United States until the era of the Protestant Revolt in order that this country, at least, could be preserved from the "contamination" of "corrupt" Catholicism. This obviously false and apparently Pharasaic interpretation of Providence was commonly expressed in early histories of American religion. *Christianity in the United States,* for example, declares: "While thirst for gold, lust of power and love of daring adventure served the Providential purpose of opening the New World to Papal Europe, and Roman Catholic colonies were successfully planted in some portions, the territory originally comprised within the United States was mysteriously guarded and reserved for another, a prepared people." [1] Lest in these latter days we mistake the religion of this "prepared people," another

[1] Dorchester, Daniel, *op. cit.,* p. 24.

superannuated history enlightens us: "In the light of events no reasoning mind can doubt that the Western Hemisphere, particularly North America, was predestined, concealed, discovered and reserved, to become the seat of a Protestant Christian nation." [2]

More recent Protestant church historians, while they persist in mentioning this invidious invention, are careful to declare that this interpretation of Providence was due to religious bias.[3] This myth is gradually being relegated to the limbo of forgotten things.

Americans are prone to picture the first English settlers as braving the perils of the deep and the lurking death of the wilderness for one, all-consuming purpose—to attain the religious liberty denied them in their habitations in the Old World. Sacrilegious though it may appear, the incontrovertible fact is that the Pilgrims, the prime exemplars of this mythology, need not have sought and did not seek in this land "freedom to worship God." This motive, as often retold in story as it is renowned in song,

[2] Clark, Joseph B., *Leavening the Nation*, p. 11. Cf. also Bacon, Leonard W., *History of American Christianity*, p. 2: "By a prodigy of divine providence the secret of the age had been kept from premature disclosure. . . . That was high strategy in the warfare for the advancement of the Kingdom of God on earth. . . . If the discovery of America had been achieved four centuries or even a century earlier, the Christianity to be transplanted to the western world would have been that of the Church of Europe at its lowest stage of decline."

[3] E.g., Sweet, William W., *Story of Religion in America* (hereafter *Story*), p. 11. Bass, Archer B., *Protestantism in the U.S.*, p. 3. The latter, however, goes on to make the very interesting statement: "However, neither the presence nor absence of any particular religious viewpoint can alter these facts: all Roman Catholic settlements prior to and including those of the 16th Century ultimately fell into dismal ruin and were, therefore, of no permanent influence. . . ."

was not included by William Bradford, the original governor of the colony, among the reasons for the Pilgrim transfer to America.[4] A recent historian writes: "Even the Pilgrims were accompanied to America by a large number of those who were influenced by other motives than soul conviction."[5] Another declares: "It is well to remember that they themselves placed the economic motive in the foreground . . . Beyond question nearly all that came to the New World came either to better their fortunes or from sheer love of adventure."[6]

Desire for freedom in religious matters was, however, a motive, if not the major factor, in the foundation of some colonies, notably Maryland, Rhode Island and Pennsylvania. While it is clear that among subsequent waves of settlers the religious freedom possible in America was of but minor importance, historians are inclined to discount the paramountcy of the desire for religious liberty even among the original immigrants.[7]

Early Protestant church leaders did urge on the settlement of America. They were, however, motivated not so much by a desire for religious liberty as by fear that the Catholic Church would gain by Protestant default control of the whole New World. The Protestant historian Sweet affirms: "Thus from the beginning of the agitation for English colonization of America to the very outbreak of

---

[4] Hart, Albert B., *American History Told by Contemporaries*, I, p. 340 ff.

[5] Andrews, Charles M., *The Colonial Period*, I, p. 65.

[6] Hall, *op. cit.*, p. 85.

[7] Hall, *op. cit.*, p. 85; Rowe, *op. cit.*, p. 9 ff.; Latourette, *op. cit.*, III, p. 190; Bates, Ernest S., *American Faith*, p. 83.

the War for Independence the Protestant crusade against Roman Catholicism was a major motive in projecting, in planting, and in extending the English colonies in America." [8]

Whatever the motives of colonization, the settlements of British America early manifested the multiplicity of denominations which was to be an outstanding characteristic of American Protestantism. The Church of England, the predecessor of the Protestant Episcopal Church, made its appearance on American shores with the settlement of Virginia. The Pilgrim Independents in Massachusetts were soon joined by the Puritan forerunners of the Congregationalists. The Dutch brought their Calvinism to New Amsterdam, the Swedes their Lutheranism to Delaware. Soon after the Catholic and some few Jews, came the German Lutherans and Evangelicals and the Scotch Presbyterians.

The fissiparous nature of American Protestantism was first demonstrated in Rhode Island, where fugitives from the Puritan theocracy of Massachusetts established the first Baptist congregation in this country.[9] The schisms that were to plague Protestantism early marked the new sect, for within a generation two rival Baptist denominations were in existence. The religious freedom accorded to Protestants quickly made Rhode Island an *omnium*

[8] Sweet, William W., *Religion in Colonial America* (hereafter *Colonial*), p. 12.

[9] For many years, that Roger Williams was one of these original Baptists was considered an established fact. Cf., e.g., Lyon, William, *A Study of the Christian Sects*, p. 88; Rowe, *op. cit.*, p. 34; Sweet, *Story*, p. 102 f. Recently, however, the truth of that belief has been questioned. Cf. Sweet, *Colonial*, p. 128.

gatherum of the Evangelical sects of the period. Within the colony were found denominations variously labeled Generalists, Fifth Monarchy Men, Antinomians, Millennialists, Familists, Anti-Sabbatarians, Arminians, Socianians, Seekers and Ranters. Nor were these the only ephemeral sects of the Colonial Period. Virginia possessed a minuscule but melodious schism from Anglicanism self-styled the Sweet Singers. Even the Quakers, who first appeared in the middle 17th Century, produced a schism which adopted the appealing though apparently meaningless title of the Contented of the God-Loving Soul.

The subsequent 18th Century witnessed the arrival of still more denominations to swell the number of the Protestant sects. The Baptists threw off several more schisms. Scotland and Northern Ireland sent Covenanters and Secessionists to join the orthodox Presbyterians already in the colonies. The German sects were augmented by the arrival of German Calvinists of the Reformed Church, Seventh Day German Baptists, Dunkers, Schwenkfelders and Moravian Brethren.

The immigration originating in the British Isles brought, together with its multitudinous sects, that intolerance so characteristic of the age.[10] In the period of settlement, most colonies enacted savage laws directed not only against Catholics but against all those who rejected the established church. Most obsessed by intolerance were the Puritan

---

[10] Metzger, Charles H., *The Quebec Act*, p. 11: "The age was in no sense a tolerant age, and these pioneers were truly children of their age . . . The victims of an obsession, these early colonists developed such a fearsomeness and such intolerance in speech and action as to cause us to wonder at the credulity and intolerance of men otherwise rational."

theocrats of Massachusetts. Of those strange people it has been written: "It is hard even for a student, and it must be for the reader, to actually realize (*sic*) how almost completely these Puritans had wiped away their Christianity and become a peculiar sect of heretical Israelites in whose doctrine there was but a tincture of Pauline theology. The symbol of the cross and of the sacraments of the cross were nowhere in New England, and the Savior walked nowhere in this New Canaan." [11] While these strictures are hard, Massachusetts had supplied their justification. For there stern bigots mulcted, whipped, branded and exiled religious dissidents; they even hanged four Quakers, who, having been exiled, ventured to return. [12]

Religious toleration, strangely enough, received its first expression from the most hated religious denomination in the colonies. [13] Maryland was founded on a policy of religious toleration. That this fundamental principle had been adopted before the colony was founded is proven by the instructions issued to his governors by Lord Baltimore before the sailing of the Ark and the Dove:

"Imprimis. His Lordship requires his said Governor & Commissioners that in their voyage to Mary Land they be very carefull to preserve unity & peace amongst all the passangers on shippboard, and that they suffer no scandall nor offense to be given to any of the Protestants, whereby

[11] MacLeod, "Contacts," p. 955.

[12] Channing, *op. cit.,* I, p. 332; Hall, *op. cit.,* p. 130.

[13] Ives, J. Moss, *The Ark and the Dove,* p. 187: "The claim to priority in the field of civil and religious liberty must after all be yielded to Maryland, for here in the early days of the colony can be found the first full recognition of the basic American principle of equality before the law."

any just complaint may heereafter be made by them in Virginea or in England; and for that end they cause all acts of Romane Catholique religion to be done as privately as may be, and that they instruct all the Romane Catholiques to be silent upon all occasions of discourse concerning matters of religion; and that the said Governor & Commissioners treate the Protestants with as much mildness and favour as justice will permitt. And this is to be observed at land as well as at sea." [14]

Baltimore, in 1636, confirmed this policy by exacting from his governor an oath that no Christian in Maryland would be disturbed because of his religious beliefs or practises. Under his instructions, the Maryland legislature, in 1649, wrote the principle of religious freedom into the State laws by the justly famed Act of Toleration.

Since this Act of Toleration had been amended to impose severe penalties on blasphemy and to exclude unitarians, the Catholic claim to priority in enunciating the principle of religious freedom in America has often been attacked as fraudulent. But as Sweet points out: "The anti-unitarian clause was not a part of the original text sent by Lord Baltimore from England, but was added by the Puritan-Protestant party in the Maryland Assembly, so as to jibe with the policy of the Long Parliament in punishing heresies and blasphemies." [15]

Yet the Act of Toleration marked the end of toleration. The practise of religious freedom had been assured, and

[14] Hughes, *op. cit.,* I (text), p. 261. Hart, *op. cit.,* I, p. 247 ff., reprints the whole document.
[15] Sweet, *Colonial,* p. 178.

legal enactments in its defense were not necessary, until Puritans, who had been expelled because of their religion from the settlements of Virginia, moved to the hospitable shores of Maryland. The Puritan in Catholic Maryland "played the part of a viper stinging the bosom that had warmed him and made the most disgraceful chapter in the history of Puritanism and religious liberty." [16] For the Calvinists repaid the generosity of Maryland by staging a revolt, seizing power, and repealing the Toleration Act. Thereafter Maryland's penal laws against Catholics were equaled in savagery only by the laws of Puritan Massachusetts.

Catholic Maryland was not alone in its advocacy of religious toleration. A generation after the Ark and the Dove had passed the Chesapeake capes, another group of pioneers sailed up the Delaware River to establish Philadelphia. Pennsylvania, under the guidance of the Quaker William Penn, was founded in 1681 as a haven where men, provided they were theists, could settle and find freedom to practise their religion without let or hindrance by the colonial government.

Two years after the foundation of Maryland, the colony of Rhode Island was begun by Roger Williams, who has been saluted as the "Apostle of Religious Toleration." Wide acceptance has been given to claims that Rhode Island granted religious toleration before Maryland, and on a wider basis than Maryland. These assertions are based on the fact that the Maryland Act of Toleration, which ex-

[16] Cobb, Sanford H., *Rise of Religious Liberty in America*, p. 378.

tended only to Trinitarians, was not passed until 1649.[17] These claims, however, cannot be accepted without reservations. When Williams was expelled from Massachusetts, he had no intention of founding a colony, nor any idea of a commonwealth based on a principle of civil and religious freedom.[18] Rhode Island was not granted its first charter, which made no mention of religious freedom, until 1644, and had no government, properly speaking, before 1647.[19] The colony continued in an unsettled condition until it received its second royal charter in 1663. While this document permitted full religious freedom to all the inhabitants of the colony, the Rhode Island legislature nullified this grant by enacting a law disfranchising all Jews and Catholics.[20] It has been asserted with some probability that this law was passed as soon as the royal charter reached the colony, in a period when Williams was still the dominant personality in the settlements.[21] No Catholic

[17] Though religious freedom in Maryland was legally restricted to Trinitarians, it appears that Jews were present in the colony and were not molested. Cf. Andrews, C., *op. cit.*, III, p. 311 n.; Andrews, Matthew P., *The Founding of Maryland,* p. 156.

[18] Ernst, James, *Roger Williams,* p. 157; Andrews, C., *op. cit.*, I, p. 421.

[19] Ernst, *op. cit.*, p. 271.

[20] Andrews, Matthew, *op. cit.*, p. 155, quotes a decision of the Rhode Island Supreme Court in 1762 denying the franchise to two Jews on the grounds that to admit them was "wholly inconsistent with the first principles upon which the colony was founded."

[21] Hall, *op. cit.*, p. 138, takes it for granted that the law was passed in 1663. Ives, *op. cit.*, p. 193, and Andrews, Matthew, *op. cit.*, p. 155, favor the early date. Strangely, Ernst, *op. cit.*, makes no mention of the law. Channing, *op. cit.*, II, p. 426: "The act was never passed in 1663-4, or at any time during the life of Roger Williams; it first appears on the statute books in 1719; how it got there no one knows." The only possible explanation, of course, is that the Rhode Island legislature passed it. Andrews, Chas., *op. cit.*, II, p. 61 declares that Rhode Island disfranchised

entered Rhode Island in Williams' lifetime, for his hatred of Catholicism was so notorious that it would be a foolhardy man who would put his alleged tolerance to the test.[22]

But while the story of bigotry and religious intolerance is an unpleasant chapter of American colonial history, it is overmatched by the colonial record of oppression of the colored races.

"To say that the English were not interested in the uplift of the enslaved Africans would hardly express the truth." [23] As the number of Negro slaves in America grew, the colonial legislatures enacted stringent measures designed to keep the colored people in subjection.[24] Slaveowners exercised over their human property an arbitrary domination unchecked by law. The manumission of slaves was a comparative rarity.

Nor did the colored people find in Protestantism an effective champion. Humane ministers, it is true, manifested an interest in Negroes, and owners motivated by Christian principles treated their slaves with kindness and instructed them in the fundaments of the Christian religion. While the economic value of the slavery system was still in doubt, a number of the smaller sects, notably the Quakers, raised their voices in condemnation of the institution. Beyond these futile protests, however, the sects spent little or no

the Catholics "in 1729"—a decade after the first statute book contained the law.

[22] Ives, op. cit., p. 192. "In the days of Roger Williams there was no sanctuary in Rhode Island for Catholics."

[23] Woodson, op. cit., p. 583.

[24] For some details of these laws, cf. Channing, op. cit., II, p. 393 f.; Woodson, op. cit., p. 567 ff.

energy in efforts to ameliorate the hard lot of the slaves. Nor were the sects deeply concerned with the evangelization of the Negroes. Few attempts were made at their conversion, and these few met but little success.[25] It need cause no wonder, then, that "Negroes often speak of the Latin races as more humane than the Teutonic; and some go so far as to say that the Catholic religion comes nearer to the teachings of Jesus than that of the Protestants. These opinions have resulted mainly from the differing experiences of Negroes in contact with these races in the Western Hemisphere. We do know that in religion, law and customs, these Caucasian elements widely differ with respect to the weaker races." [26]

The Negro slave could hope that his life, valuable to his master, would be protected; the Indian in British America had no such hope. With historical accuracy did Mark Twain declare that the English colonists fell first on their knees and then on the aborigines. While there were some rare manifestations, notably in Quaker Pennsylvania, of justice and charity towards the savages, the common colonial opinion has been summed up in the phrase, "the only good Indian is a dead one." The history of the colonial frontier is largely a record of efforts to make the Indians "good." When the white man's diseases, to which the aborigines had no resistance, periodically decimated the Indian population, there were not lacking colonists who considered the dread visitations special assistance granted

---

[25] Latourette, *op. cit.*, III, p. 225, devotes but a single paragraph of his huge work to Protestant efforts to evangelize the Negroes.

[26] Woodson, *op. cit.*, p. 583.

them by Divine Providence.[27] Nor did the English hesitate to second the efforts of Providence by massacre and by slave-raiding, a practise which persisted in British America for nearly two hundred years after it had been abolished in Spanish America.[28]

The annihilation of the Indians went on unchecked by Protestantism. Indeed, MacLeod declares: "In none of the New England colonies, not even in Roger Williams' Rhode Island, was there evident even a sincere desire on the part of officials, clergy, or lay leaders, to see the Indians established or absorbed as Christian communities. The official spirit is actually, I honestly believe, after long study of the original records, summed up in the spirit which led a Mather in 1676, after a wanton massacre of 600 virtually helpless Indians, to enter the pulpit of the leading Congregational church in Boston and (in his own words) "thank God that this day we have sent 600 heathen souls to hell." [29]

Protestantism, on the whole, manifested a singular apathy towards the evangelization of the aborigines. While the missionaries of New Spain and New France were numbered in the thousands, the missionaries of British America were, at most, but a few score, and the successful Protestant missions could easily be counted on the fingers of one hand.

[27] MacLeod, *American Indian Frontier*, p. 49: "An attitude peculiar to the English colonists of North America, but taken most seriously by the Puritans, was that God had sent disease in advance of Christian colonization in order to wipe out the pagan population and thereby make room for His own people . . . A variant opinion . . . maintained that God did all this spreading of disease to relieve the English of the necessity of killing off Indians by fire and sword . . ."

[28] MacLeod, "Contacts," p. 849.

[29] *Ibid*, p. 887.

Probably the most successful Protestant venture in point of numbers of mission Indians was the work of John Eliot among the tribes of Massachusetts. His mission lasted less than thirty years, claimed at its peak about 2,500 Indians, was destroyed in King Philip's War (1676), and was never successfully reestablished.[30] A notable exception to the ephemeral Protestant efforts was the mission station of Martha's Vineyard. On this Massachusetts island, a single family, the Mayhews, carried on mission work from 1641 to 1806.[31] Since the Indians were never numerous—in 1806 there were but three hundred—the Mayhew mission is noteworthy chiefly for the apostolic devotion of a single family.

A century after the establishment of Protestantism in America, there could be found at most a few hundred Protestant Indians.[32] In the 18th Century, a few more scattered attempts were made, chiefly by the non-English colonists. German Evangelicals converted a few hundred Delaware Indians who accepted the pacificism of their instructors and who consequently were massacred unresistingly by the "Scotch-Irish" Calvinists of Pennsylvania. With this sad story, the record of Colonial Protestant Indian Missions closes. Sweet writes with justice: "Although there were a few devoted and successful missionaries like John Eliot, the Mayhews and the Moravian Brethren, Colonial Protestantism as a whole was little interested in the Christianization of the infidel, and their missionary

[30] Latourette, *op. cit.,* III, p. 218.
[31] *Ibid,* p. 218.
[32] MacLeod, "Contacts," p. 888.

record was much less impressive than that of the Catholic missionaries in the Spanish and French colonies." [33]

While Protestantism was making its few futile attempts to convert the Indians, it was achieving a greater measure of liberty for its sects in the colonies. Before the close of the 17th Century, the dissenting Protestant denominations enjoyed in most of the colonies if not religious freedom— the equality of all religions before the law—at least religious toleration, the right to practise their religion without interference by the colonial governments.

A number of factors facilitated the growth of toleration for dissident Protestants. The mere multiplicity of sects was a powerful and permanent influence. The general religious apathy epidemic before 1700 weakened the opposition of the established sects to the relaxation of religious restrictions.[34] The religious effects of the so-called "Glorious Revolution" strongly influenced the policy of the colonial governments. The first Parliament of William and Mary in 1689 enacted an Act of Toleration, extending freedom of worship to all Christians, "except Papists." In the same year, the governors of the Royal colonies were instructed to extend the provisions of the act to their territories. Massachusetts, which had already permitted non-Congregational sects within its borders, received, in 1691, a new charter guaranteeing toleration to all religions except the Catholic. In 1696 South Carolina, whose example was fol-

[33] Sweet, *Colonial*, p. 9. For an interesting comparison of Protestant versus Jesuit missions, cf. Dorchester, *op. cit.*, p. 190 ff.

[34] Hall, *op. cit.*, p. 139: "What really most effectively advanced religious freedom was the growing religious indifference, of which complaints are early heard in all quarters."

lowed by North Carolina, extended liberty of conscience
to all, again "except Papists." New York, in 1691, legalized
the presence of all religions, except the Catholic Church.
Shortly after 1700, Connecticut tolerated dissenting Protestants, but not Catholics. The 1732 charter of Georgia
followed the example of the other colonies in guaranteeing
liberty of conscience to all, except the universally excepted
Catholics.[35]

But while the dissenting Protestant sects were gaining
toleration, the legal measures against Catholics were
strengthened. In 1700, Massachusetts changed the legal
penalty imposed on any "Jesuit or seminary priest" discovered in the colony from perpetual banishment to life
imprisonment. New York in the same year passed an
identical law, and, in 1741, executed Margaret Kerry, "a
profest Papist," and John Ury, erroneously suspected of
being a Catholic priest.[36] The laws of Maryland formed
possibly the most comprehensive code against Catholicism.
In 1715 that originally Catholic colony disfranchised Catholics, and, in 1740, made it a capital offense to reconcile
lapsed Catholics to the Church. Nor did Maryland neglect
economic sanctions. All land owned by Catholics was sub-
jected to a double tax, and apostate Catholics were given
the legal right to seize the estates of their Catholic parents.[37]

The penal acts of the colonial legislatures against Catholi-

[35] On these charters and laws, cf. Hughes, *op. cit.,* II (text), p. 161 f.;
Hall, *op. cit.,* p. 130 f.; O'Gorman, *op. cit.,* p. 234 f.; Guilday, Peter K.,
John England, I, p. 134 f.; Nevins, Allen, *American States during and
after the Revolution,* p. 424 f.

[36] Hughes, *op. cit.,* II (text), p. 184.

[37] On the laws of Maryland, cf. Hughes, *loc. cit.,* Channing, *op. cit.,* II,
p. 424 ff.

cism were buttressed by a well-conditioned public opinion, for throughout the colonial period the press and the pulpit launched unceasing vitriolic attacks against the "Scarlet Woman of Rome." [38] Sweet affirms that: "The vast output of this type of propaganda in the colonies is almost unbelievable." [39]

Under such circumstances, Catholicism did not hold its own. It is not surprising that people, lacking opportunities for the practise of their religion, hated, feared and penalized because they were guilty of the crime of being Catholics, should drift away from the Catholic Church. Most of the Catholics who settled in British America before the War for Independence did in fact abandon their religion. Estimates of the numbers lost to Catholicism throughout the colonial period vary from 100,000 to 250,000 and even higher.[40] When the conflict between England and her American colonies developed into war, barely 25,000 Catholics could be found in the Thirteen Colonies.

While Catholics weak in their faith were relinquishing their religion, Protestantism was plagued by indifference.[41] Large numbers of nominal Protestants manifested little interest in religious matters and allowed their connections with the sects to lapse.

In the middle of the 18th Century, however, Protestantism regained the allegiance of large numbers of Americans

---

[38] Cf. the compilation of Ray, M. A., *American Opinion of Roman Catholicism in the 18th Century*, p. 63 ff., p. 165 ff.

[39] Sweet, *Colonial*, p. 12.

[40] For a study of this Catholic leakage, cf. Guilday, *England*, I, p. 7 ff.; Shaughnessy, *op. cit.*, p. 52 ff.

[41] Sweet, *Colonial*, p. 271 f.; Hall, *op. cit.*, p. 139.

through a movement known as the "Great Awakening." This return to organized religion occurred coincidentally with the rise of Methodism in England under the leadership of John Wesley, and was influenced by it. Although Methodism, destined to be one of the largest and most influential of American denominations, had no organized congregation in this country until 1766, its founder, one of the purest and greatest figures Protestantism has produced, spent some time in Georgia a score of years before.[42] Though his American experiences—he had an unhappy love-affair, and fled the colonies in circumstances which led to his vilification and a libel suit [43]—were disheartening, Wesley lived to see his Methodism accepted by ever increasing numbers of Americans.

The most prominent leaders of the Great Awakening were Jonathan Edwards and George Whitefield. Edwards, the greatest name among colonial theologians, founded a new school of theology, which, though basically Calvinistic, began the mitigation of the harsher Genevan doctrines. Whitefield, considered the greatest English pulpit orator of the 18th Century, made evangelical tours of the country five times between 1740 and 1770, dying here on his last visit.

The Great Awakening introduced to the American scene

[42] Wesley's Methodism revivified the dying Protestantism of England. After his death, his followers showed their Protestantism by breaking away from the Church of England, forming their own organization, and at once dividing into a number of schisms. Even before Wesley's death, Whitefield led a group out of Wesley's movement in a fundamental disagreement over Calvinistic predestination. To Wesley's honor, he defended the milder Arminian faith.

[43] Piette, Maximin, *John Wesley,* p. 298 ff.

one of the most remarkable and characteristic phenomena of American religious history, the revival. This Protestant institution was the greatest single factor in the large growth of Evangelical Protestantism throughout the 18th and 19th Centuries.[44]

Through the long history of the revival, the procedure followed varied but little. Since the object attained was the emotional "conversion" of the people, the revival and its methods were quickly adopted by the Evangelicals. From a pulpit in the church or a platform under the open skies, a minister or series of exhorters would lead the congregation in the singing of highly emotional hymns, utter prayers surcharged with feeling and shout exhortations vividly colored with hell-fire and brimstone. "Sinners" would be urged to mount the "mourners' bench" or the "anxious seat," be "convinced of sin" and "accept the Lord."

Due to the intense emotional stress which the revivals engendered, rather repugnant acts and scenes were of frequent occurrence.[45] Instances of hysteria were considered visitations of the Holy Spirit and were, apparently, sought deliberately by both ministers and congregations.[46] Fre-

[44] Douglass, H. Paul, *Church Unity Movements in the U.S.*, p. 34: "For two hundred years, a conventional type of revivalism was the chief external feature of American Protestantism."

[45] Cf. Mecklin, *op. cit.*, p. 250 ff.; Loud, Grover C., *Evangelized America*, p. 23 ff. Fuller details of this revival hysteria will be found in the discussion of the frontier revivals.

[46] Hall, *op. cit.*, p. 153: ". . . Jonathan Edwards himself had to protest against the demand for physical contortions and hysteria as evidence of the movings of the Holy Spirit."

Piette, *op. cit.*, p. 381 ff., gives some examples of hysteria in similar meetings in England, conducted by Wesley, who also attributed this hysteria to the Holy Spirit.

quently the emotional orgy of the revival was continued for days and nights on end, until the emotional resources of the congregation had been completely exhausted.

Though some ministers of non-Evangelical sects participated in the revivals, the majority bitterly opposed the Great Awakening. Nor was their acrimony lessened by Evangelical gains in church membership occasionally registered at their expense. Typical of the opinion of the leaders of the middle class sects are these words of an Episcopalian minister on Whitefield and a subsequent exhorter:

"It would be an endless attempt to describe the scenes of confusion and disturbance occasioned by him; the divisions of families, neighborhoods and towns, . . . the undutifulness of children and servants, . . . the disorders of the night. . . . In many communities, several preaching and several exhorting and praying at the same time; the rest crying or laughing, yelping, sprawling or fainting. This revel in some places has been maintained many days and nights together."

"After him came one Tennant, a monster! impudent and noisy, and told them all they were dam'd, dam'd, dam'd; this charmed them, and in the most dreadful winter I ever saw, people wallowed in the snow night and day for the benefit of his beastly brayings, and many ended their days under these fatigues." [47]

The period of the Great Awakening terminated with the death of Whitefield in 1770. The movement had increased the church membership of the Evangelical sects, particularly those of the Baptists. It had supplied Evangelicalism with a spirit and a tested method with which it was to dominate

[47] Clark, *op. cit.*, p. 114; Platner, *op. cit.*, p. 225.

the frontier Christianity of the 19th Century and to gain numerical preeminence in American Protestantism. By way of reaction, the Great Awakening caused bitter controversies within the sects. Revulsion to the emotional orgies and the abuses consequent to the revivals sowed the seeds of many future schisms; and the repulsion caused by the Awakening instigated a reappraisal of the doctrines on which it was based and gave impetus to the movement seeking the liberalization of the orthodox Protestant theology.[48]

But religious problems were tabled while the question of political independence was debated with England.

[48] Hall, *op. cit.*, pp. 165-166: "Many had been very much repelled (by the Great Awakening), and the rise of a skeptical and questioning type of Protestantism may be dated from this repulsion."

CHAPTER IV

FREEDOM AND ORGANIZATION

I
T IS no longer the fashion to attribute the growth of the
American demand for independence from England to
the logical development of the principles of the Protestant
Revolt in the churches of this country. While it will not be
denied that the ideology of the American Revolution derived from principles long since evolved or adopted by
Christian philosophers, it can be very seriously doubted
that these principles were peculiarly Protestant or, more
particularly, Puritan.[1]

Nor did organized Protestantism play, as a whole, any
decisive role either in fostering the principles of the Revolution or in sustaining the patriots through the dark days
of the wearisome conflict.[2] While some influential Protes-

[1] Some Catholics like to think that the principles underlying the Revolution were taken directly from Scholastic philosophers. The evidence
behind this claim, however, is weak. For a discussion of the remote
influence of Scholasticism, cf. Ryan, John A. and Millar, Moorhouse, *State
and Church,* p. 118 ff.

[2] Hall, *op. cit.,* p. 166: "To claim therefore, as once it was the fashion
to do, that the sturdy 'Puritan' love of liberty was the sustaining cause of
the war is unhistoric. Even using the word Puritan loosely to cover the
dissenting tradition in its various manifestations it is not true that the war
can be traced in any sense to their love of independence. The real Puritan
had no love of any liberty except what he himself needed in order to
force the Kingdom of God upon men, as he was commanded by God
to do."

tant ministers advocated the colonial cause, a very large proportion of the Protestant clergy maintained a neutral position or declared for British rule. At the outbreak of open warfare, for example, the majority of the Anglican parsons took flight for England.[3] Hall declares: "It can only be noted by the historian that at the time of the war, organized religion was exceedingly uninfluential, and was far too divided to exercise a decisive influence on either side of the question in controversy . . . As it was, neither the dissenting bodies nor the Anglo-Catholic Church nor anything that can properly be called Puritanism played any great part in bringing on the war or forcing it to a final issue." [4]

Yet two issues involving religion, or rather opposition to a specific religion, were of importance in the origins of the Revolution. The first was a widespread colonial opposition to the Church of England, which since it was regarded as preparing the way for "Popery" through its "Prelacy," was hated by the Evangelicals only less than the Catholic Church. The mere proposal that an Anglican bishopric be established in the colonies led to American outcries which linked the devil, Rome and Whitehall in one sentence.[5] Yet this dread of Prelacy, while it fostered opposition to the English King and Parliament, was more a factor conditioning the Americans for the future war than a direct cause of the war.

But the colonials, stirred to anger by the proposal of an

[3] *Ibid*, p. 171.
[4] *Ibid*, p. 176.
[5] Miller, John C., *Origins of the American Revolution*, p. 187 ff.

English prelate in America, rose in arms when England appeared as the protector of "Popery." The Quebec Act, which guaranteed toleration to Catholicism in Canada, has been called an outstanding religious cause of the American Revolution. While the territorial clauses of the legislative measure were disliked, Metzger sums up the evidence: "Thus it appears that the Quebec Act was one of the outstanding grievances of the American colonists, and that the religious section of the bill, rather than the political, aroused fear and resentment." [6]

The hatred and fear of Catholicism which had long been fostered by Protestant ministers reached its apogee after the passage of this Act. Political propagandists seized upon it as "their juiciest plum since the Stamp Act." [7] The pulpit, the press, local legislative assemblies, popular songs and verse vied in picturing the dread horrors of the Papal triumph, imminent unless patriots resisted it.[8] Miller writes that the Quebec Act, perhaps more than any other act of the British government, made possible the victory of the radicals and made the people "generally ripe for any plan the Congress (might) advise, should it be war itself." [9]

This colonial opposition to Catholicism brought about one of the strangest paradoxes in history. While the Thirteen Colonies, some of them British and Protestant for a century and a half, were waging war against their

[6] Metzger, *op. cit.,* p. 90.

[7] Miller, *op. cit.,* p. 373.

[8] Metzger, *op. cit.,* p. 37 ff., gives numerous quotations from the sources. Cf. Miller, *op. cit.,* p. 373 ff.; p. 457 ff.; Shea, John G., *History of the Catholic Church in the U.S.,* II, p. 137 ff.; Ray, *op. cit.,* p. 262 ff.

[9] Miller, *op. cit.,* p. 376.

mother country, the only possession on the North American continent which remained faithful to the British Crown was Canada, French and Catholic, and subject to England less than a decade and a half.

When the Continental Congress assembled in 1775, one of its first acts was to dispatch an Address to the People of Great Britain calculated to stir up anti-Catholic bigotry as a weapon against the British government.[10] Later, in a bit of diplomatic double-dealing, Congress sent to the inhabitants of Canada an irenic address, carefully omitting all anti-Catholic sentiments, which appealed for their assistance against England. Neither this address nor the later Congressional emissaries to Canada achieved success. Canada had already been informed of the Address to the People of Great Britain, and had had long experience with American hatred of all things Catholic. When the choice between the Colonies and Britain was presented, the Canadian Catholic clergy "never doubted for a moment from which of the two warring parties to expect the greater meed of tolerance and freedom. The bishop himself was quick to give the lead." [11] The decisive element in the Canadian choice was very probably the unfortunate address to the English. Shea declares: "All Canada would have been won but for the influence of John Jay's bigoted Address to the People of Great Britain, in which the Canadians and their religion were assailed in the grossest terms.[12]

The early days of the Revolution saw no lessening of

---

[10] Cf. Metzger, *op. cit.*, p. 151 ff.

[11] Coupland, Reginald, *The Quebec Act*, p. 170.

[12] Shea, *op. cit.*, II, p. 145. Cf. Miller, *op. cit.*, p. 457.

the anti-Catholic spirit. Some colonies, as in the days of the French and Indian Wars, disarmed all Catholics within their borders, fearing by some strange paradox that the Catholics would fight for the preservation of English rule and her anti-Catholic penal laws. Inasmuch as the Catholics had but fifty of the more than 3,000 religious congregations organized in the colonies, it is apparent that even if the Catholics had upheld the cause of the Crown, they could have accomplished little.[13]

Yet at long last forces were in operation which were to gain toleration in America for the Catholic Church. The address directed to the people of Canada and the mission sent to withdraw them from their allegiance to the English King were but the first diplomatic moves made by the Congress which ultimately forced Americans to recognize the expediency, scarcely based on high moral principles, of extending toleration to Catholicism.

The advance of this tolerance was furthered by the support which the Catholic colonists contributed to the cause of the Colonies. In contradistinction to the Protestant ministry, no Catholic priest in the Colonies gave support to the British. The Catholic laity supplied their full share of officers and soldiers to the Continental forces, and made their influence felt in the field of diplomacy and politics. The Catholic Indians of Maine and of the Old Northwest were among the few groups of aborigines who rallied to the patriot cause.[14] This wholehearted Catholic support could not but mitigate the colonial anti-Catholicism.

[13] Sweet, *Story*, p. 251; Metzger, *op. cit.*, p. 8.
[14] Shea, *op. cit.*, II, p. 154 ff.

American diplomacy, in quest of aid from Catholic countries, forbade the alienation of French and Spanish opinion through anti-Catholic sentiment or demonstrations in the new States. The observance of Guy Fawkes Day, which was celebrated by hanging the Pope in effigy, was forbidden to the Army by Washington. On several occasions after French intervention in the struggle, Congress diplomatically attended Catholic services. The presence of large numbers of French soldiers and sailors did much to drive the American anti-Catholicism underground.

While, therefore, in the days of Lexington and Concord, "nowhere in British America were the Catholics wholly immune from religious disadvantages," [15] the developments of the revolutionary years had so assisted the Catholics that "by 1789 all obstacles to the Catholic worship had been done away with in all the states." [16] It is clear, however, that "toleration, when it did come, came not as the result of any high-minded principle of liberty, but accidentally as a compromise or by-product of the policy which was brought into being with the Revolution." [17] Nor must it be forgotten that Catholicism was accorded toleration, and not freedom; Catholics in many of the States were still, because of their religion, only citizens of the second rank.

In the first flush of independence, Delaware, Pennsylvania and Maryland adopted constitutions guaranteeing

[15] Nevins, *op. cit.,* p. 421.
[16] Fiske, John, *The Critical Period,* p. 87.
[17] Guilday, Peter K., "The Catholic Church in the United States," *Thought,* I (1926), p. 8.

equality before the law to all Christians.[18] Pennsylvania, however, did not extend this freedom to non-Christians until 1790, while Delaware till 1793 required that all office-holders be Trinitarians. Perhaps the presence of a French army and the French fleet was more than a minor factor when "Rhode Island nobly distinguished herself by contrast when, in 1784, she extended the franchise to Catholics."[19] In 1786 Virginia guaranteed religious freedom to all by enacting Thomas Jefferson's famous Bill of Rights. The new State of Vermont, in 1793, approved a constitution guaranteeing full religious freedom. In 1798 Georgia removed the last religious discriminations from its statutes.

In the remaining states, however, full religious freedom was not achieved until the 19th Century. South Carolina, after a brief establishment of Protestantism as the state religion, declared for religious freedom in 1808. Connecticut disestablished the Congregational Church in 1818. New York, which had forbidden the naturalization of Catholics and had restricted offices to non-Catholics, repealed its last anti-Catholic laws in 1821. Massachusetts relinquished the practise of collecting tithes from both Catholics and dissenting Protestants for the support of the Congregational Church and, in 1833, terminated the establishment of that denomination. The religious tests for office-holders were removed in 1835 by North Carolina and, in 1844, by New Jersey. While New Hampshire, in 1819, passed a belated Toleration Act, applicable only to Christians, it did not

---

[18] For these state constitutions, cf. Thorpe, Francis N. (ed), *The Federal and State Constitutions.*
[19] Fiske, *op. cit.,* p. 77.

remove its constitutional restrictions on Catholics until 1877.[20]

In the light of these facts, to claim that the Revolution brought religious freedom as an immediate consequence is in direct contravention of the evidence. Since fifty years after Yorktown religious freedom was not guaranteed by several American states, the most that can be justly claimed for the Revolution is that it established religious toleration and set in motion causes which led ultimately to religious freedom.

In the critical period immediately consequent to the Revolutionary War, the need of unity was felt in the churches as well as in the states. No major church had achieved organization on a national basis before the termination of the war. Some were ruled by bishops or synods in Europe; the majority, being of a congregational polity, were governed by members of the local congregations. Shortly after the close of the war, there was a general movement among the churches in the direction of organizations on national lines.

The Catholics in the Thirteen Colonies had been located under the supervision of the Vicar Apostolic of London. Since the continuance of his leadership would have been in conflict with patriotic feelings, an American ecclesiastical superior had to be provided for the Church in America. While agitation for an American Catholic bishop had begun among the colonial Catholics as early as 1756, the

[20] For further details, cf. Channing, *op. cit.*, V, p. 210; Shea, *op. cit.*, II, p. 160 f. Silcox and Fisher, *op. cit.*, p. 84: "In New Hampshire, there still remains some vestiges of the ancient relation between Church and State in the present constitution . . ."

Church, mindful of the American hatred of "prelacy," moved slowly in the erection of a national hierarchy.[21] The lack of interest shown by the public in the bishops of the new Protestant Episcopal Church allayed Catholic apprehensions, and the Catholic Church in America was given its first American ecclesiastical superior. John Carroll was appointed successively Prefect Apostolic, Vicar Apostolic, and finally, in 1789, Bishop of the see of Baltimore. The government of his huge diocese, comprising all the territories of the United States, was simplified by the concentration in enclaves in Maryland and Pennsylvania of the majority of the 35,000 Catholics present in the United States in 1790. The homogeneous composition of the laity, the majority descended from migrants from the British Isles, and of the clergy, all former members of the suppressed Society of Jesus, further eased the difficulties of his task. As the numbers of Catholics multiplied in the 19th Century, the national organization was rapidly developed and expanded. A century after the erection of the first episcopal see, the Catholic Church in the United States was organized in seventy-nine dioceses.

The close of the Revolutionary era found the American Anglican Church in a difficult position. Patriots viewed with suspicion its connections with the Established Church of England, especially since the majority of the Anglican clergy felt it prudent to leave the country during the war with England. Nevertheless, the remaining clergy bravely set about the work of reorganization. Upon the refusal

---

[21] Cf. Hughes, *op. cit.*, II (text), p. 566 ff.; Shearer, Donald, *Pontificia Americana*, p. 75 ff.

of the Anglican episcopate to consecrate bishops for the new church, the first episcopal ordinations were performed by Scotch non-juring bishops in 1784; and three years later, after a reversal of policy, the Archbishop of Canterbury conferred episcopal orders on American candidates. In 1789 the new church adopted a constitution. This document contained several novelties: the new denomination assumed the title of the "Protestant Episcopal Church," the Prayer Book received several necessary alterations (the prayers for the King, for example, were dropped), and the laity received a large share of the direction of the church.

The Calvinistic churches had developed their organizations along with the Catholics and the Anglicans. Even before the outbreak of the Revolutionary War, Scotch Secessionist and Covenanter Presbyterians had organized synods and had foreshadowed the progress of American Protestantism by merger and schism. In 1788 the regular Presbyterians organized the major Presbyterian denomination, now known as the Presbyterian Church of the United States of America.[22] Till the end of the colonial period, the Dutch and German Calvinists had been under the supervision of the Classis (Synod) of Amsterdam. Several Dutch congregations had severed the bonds with Europe by 1775; after the war, all the local churches broke their connection with the Amsterdam Classis. In 1793 the Dutch created the Reformed Church in America, and the Germans erected the Reformed Church in the United States. These two sects furnished another prognosis of Protestant development in

[22] The full title of this denomination is necessary to distinguish it from its schismatic offspring, the Presbyterian Church in the United States.

America, the predilection for national particularism over church unity.

The desire for a national organization developed more slowly among the Lutherans. A number of Swedish congregations, in fact, relinquished Lutheranism to cast in their lot with the new Protestant Episcopal Church. Only in 1820 was the General Synod of the Lutheran Church in America established by the German Lutherans.

The congregational policy of the Evangelical sects militated against the national organization of those denominations. The Quakers remained steadfast in their congregationalism and, partly as a result of this policy, the Friends became a very minor numerical group in American Protestantism. Other Evangelical sects, while maintaining the principle of congregationalism, approximated national unity through the establishment of powerful property-holding foreign mission boards or conventions. Thus the regular Baptist congregations achieved a loose confederation by the establishment of a national convention in 1814, and a board of foreign missions, largely under Congregational control, prepared the way for a national federation of Congregational churches after the Civil War.

One noteworthy exception to the congregationalism of the Evangelical denominations was the new Methodist Episcopal Church. The connection of the Methodists with the Anglican Church and the exodus of the Methodist ministers to England reduced the nascent church to dire straits during the Revolution.[23] At the close of the war, but a few scattered handfuls of Methodists could be found

[23] Hall, *op. cit.*, p. 196.

in the colonies. Under inspiring leadership, however, Methodism came out of eclipse as one of the most vital forces in American Protestantism. While Wesley, true to his ministry in the Anglican Church, kept his British followers in the English Establishment, his objections to the creation of an independent American Methodist church were overcome by the success of the American Revolution and the consequent impossibility of applying his British policy to America. Putting aside his doubts of his powers to ordain priests or consecrate bishops, he performed a ceremony of ordination over American "superintendents." [24] These men, who adopted the title of "bishop" in the United States, assumed control of the minuscule American congregations, established the new church on a firm foundation, and brought about a remarkable early expansion of church membership. The greatest single factor in this early development was the laborious life of Francis Asbury, one of these first Methodist bishops. Among the greatest churchmen in the history of America, and the first of the famed Methodist "circuit-riders," Asbury worked prodigiously in the interests of his church. Before his death in 1816, he had travelled over 300,000 difficult miles, preached 16,000 sermons, ordained 4,000 Methodist ministers, and witnessed Methodist church membership increase from 300 to about 200,000.

As the churches organized, the stirrings of a new movement which was to change the very foundations of Protestantism in this country were noticeable in some of the older denominations. Many factors contributed to the new theo-

[24] Piette, *op. cit.*, p. 386.

logical trend.[25] The widespread influence of rationalistic and naturalistic philosophies, the doctrines of English Deism and French Jacobinism, the cult of humanitarianism, the epidemic contempt for religious creeds, traditions, and authority: doctrinal controversies and sectarian conflicts, the reaction to the Great Awakening and its stress on emotionalism over doctrine, the continuing opposition to the harsh Calvinistic theology—all gave impetus to the growth of a theology denying the fundamental doctrines of Protestant orthodoxy. The erstwhile Puritan churches of New England were the first to feel the effects of the new theology. By the end of the 18th Century ministers of Unitarian tendencies occupied the pulpits of many of the most influential Congregational churches, and Universalist preachers were gathering congregations.[26] While in the subsequent century the Evangelical sects were to impose their early orthodoxy on the frontier, Arminianism continued its penetration of the Calvinistic sects and prepared the way for the widespread acceptance of the new liberal theology.

[25] Cf. Parrington, Vernon L., *Main Currents in American Thought*, II, p. 322 ff.; Haroutunian, Joseph, *Piety versus Moralism,* p. 177 ff, *et passim*.

[26] So many Massachusetts Congregationalists rejected the doctrine of regeneration that the saying became common that "One born in Boston need not be born again."

CHAPTER V

THE FRONTIER

THE great migration to the West, continuing from the latter years of the American Revolution to the Civil War, was not only a movement of major importance in the political and social history of the United States, but one of the greatest significance in the history of American religion. When the peak of migration had passed, the Evangelical sects had emerged as the dominant denominations in American Protestantism. Two prime factors explain the tremendous expansion of Evangelicalism on the frontier. The message and the methods of the Evangelical sects were very well adapted to the prevailing conditions of frontier life.[1] And Evangelicalism had the field practically to itself.

Few non-Evangelical denominations made major efforts to evangelize the frontier. In the early 19th Century, the Catholic Church had neither the men nor the means to spare for the task; its efforts perforce were concentrated on the construction of the Church in the Eastern cities. With the exception of some Presbyterian groups, the churches of Anglican, Lutheran and Calvinist provenance

[1] Channing, *op. cit.,* V, p. 221: "Conditions on the frontier . . . were favorable to the peculiar influences and modes of procedure of the Baptists and the Methodists and, to a lesser degree, of the Presbyterians."

let slip the opportunity to retain the allegiance of their members on the frontier and to gain the adhesion of the frontier masses.

In the opening years of the migration, the initial gains to organized Protestantism were made by the older sects. The "Scotch-Irish" Presbyterians of the frontier gained many recruits for their denomination from the newcomers. The growth of Presbyterianism was aided by the Congregationalists. In 1801 the two sects drew up a "Plan of Union," by the terms of which members of the two churches were to organize in each new settlement a single congregation with a minister of either "persuasion" to officiate at divine services. In almost every instance, the operation of the plan fostered the growth of Presbyterianism at the expense of the Puritan sect. It is estimated that the application of this covenant cost the New England church the loss of 2,000 congregations.[2]

As the 19th Century progressed, however, the initial Presbyterian advantages disappeared. Whole presbyteries seceded from the Calvinist church, the Springfield presbytery to be a forerunner of the Disciples of Christ and the Cumberland to set itself up as an independent denomination. Yet the major reason for this recession of Presbyterianism was not the loss of the schismatic presbyteries, but the comparative unsuitability of the sect for frontier conditions when faced with competition from the Evangelicals.

The frontier provided an environment most suitable for the rapid growth of Evangelicalism. Frontier life was rough, passions were elemental, reactions were emotional

[2] Neve, *op. cit.,* p. 498.

rather than intellectual. Frontiersmen generally were of the lower economic classes, poor and poorly educated. Their means of recreation, of emotional outlet, were limited. They were ripe for the revival.

The Methodist and Baptist sects were, at the time, equipped to satisfy the emotional demands of the pioneers.[3] Both were Evangelical, both emphasized the "conversion" and stressed strongly the emotional quality of their faiths, both hesitated not to recruit perfervid ministers from the ranks of the uneducated frontiersmen.[4]

The Arminian theology of the Methodists appealed to the individualism of the pioneers; their episcopal polity, though in conflict with the democratic tendencies of the borderland, and the cause of many later schisms, gave centralized direction to the work of evangelization; their circuit riders were admirably adapted to serve the frontier's scattered communities. The congregational polity of the Baptists suited the democratic frontiersmen; the absence of any defined Baptist doctrines, save the peculiar insistence on baptism by immersion, met the approval of the undogmatic pioneers; the promotion of illiterate exhorters to the Baptist ministry appealed to the primitive egalitarianism of the borderlands. Indeed, the frontier Baptists developed a "deep-seated prejudice against educated and salaried min-

---

[3] Bates, *op. cit.*, p. 327: "Methodism was adapted to appeal both to the most generous impulses and the most benighted prejudices of the American frontiersman." Cf. Hall, *op. cit.*, p. 198.

[4] Bates, *op. cit.*, p. 329: "The requirements for the clergy were steadily lowered until they could be met by anyone with a native talent for exhortation." *Ibid*, p. 332: "The real ground of appeal was the emotionalism which was present in equal amount in the faith of both sects."

isters." [5] This prejudice, when later middle-class Baptists sought to elevate the educational standards of the clergy, led to several schisms. [6] Methodist competition for the frontier masses affected the theological trends of the frontier Baptists. The Arminian proclivities within the denomination were checked, and Calvinism was reaffirmed.

The closing years of the 18th Century witnessed the initial successes of the two denominations in the borderlands west of the Alleghanies. Both groups gained large numbers of adherents in the Dark and Bloody Ground. After this test of their methods and their appeal, these champions of Evangelicalism moved on with the moving frontier. While neither sect neglected any portion of the borderlands, the Baptists devoted their major energies to the territories of the West and Southwest and the Methodists directed their main endeavors to the Northwest.

The revival was the major method and the most prominent feature in the Evangelical conquest of the frontier. Here came into existence a further development of the well-tested methods of the revival, the "camp meeting." The temporary open-air pulpits of the exhorters were surrounded by the wagons and tents of the frontier families, which had traveled, in many instances for several days, to participate in the religious and social activities of the revival. Frequently these camp meetings were attended by throngs numbering thousands. One of the earliest of

[5] Sweet, *Story*, p. 314. Many years later, Charles G. Finney, one of the most notable frontier exhorters could write in his *Memoirs*, p. 88: "For I am still solemnly impressed with the conviction that the schools are to a great extent spoiling the ministers."

[6] Clark, *op. cit.*, p. 240.

such meetings attracted crowds variously estimated as containing between 10,000 and 20,000 people.[7] At some meetings the exhorters, representing various denominations, were present by the scores.[8] Most commonly, the activities of the camp meeting would be drawn out over a period of several days.

The basis of these revivals was emotionalism.[9] Mass hysteria, deliberately induced by the exhorters and sought by the congregations, was a very common occurrence.[10] A camp meeting scene described by an eye-witness may be taken as typical: ". . . The impassioned exhortations, the earnest prayers, the sobs, shrieks, or shouts, bursting from persons under intense agitation of mind; the sudden spasms which seized upon scores, and unexpectedly dashed them to the ground—all conspired to invest the scene with terrific interest, and to work up the feelings to the highest pitch of excitement." [11]

Several types of individual or mass hysteria were especially common at the camp meetings. Possibly the most frequent casualties in this spiritual warfare were the "slain,"

[7] McMaster, John B., *History of the People of the United States,* II, p. 580.

[8] Cartwright, Peter, *Autobiography,* p. 45.

[9] Bates, *op. cit.,* p. 338 stresses strongly one fundamental emotion: "The sexual basis of the revivalist and camp meeting orgies is too obvious to be overlooked . . . When the repressed natural impulses could be dammed up no longer, they found expression in the excitement of the camp meeting, where, with howlings and rollings and sexual convulsions, souls were converted to God."

[10] Latourette, *op. cit.,* IV, p. 193, avers that "some" of the meetings were conducted without the occurrence of mass hysteria.

[11] Quoted in Sweet, *Story,* p. 331. Cf. Werner, M. R., *Brigham Young,* p. 54 ff.

people who, in the pitch of emotional excitement, lost control of their bodies and fell to the ground. At one revival, during which about 3,000 people were "slain," the afflicted men and women fell in such numbers that, "it became impossible for the multitudes to move about without trampling them, and they were hurriedly moved to the meeting house. At no time was the floor less than half covered. Some lay quiet, unable to move or speak . . . Some talked, but could not move. Some beat the floor with their heels. Some shrieking in agony, bounded about, it is said, like a live fish out of water. Many lay down and rolled over and over for hours at a time . . ." [12]

Another very common example of mass hysteria was "the jerks," which have been thus described: "The jerks" began in the head and spread rapidly to the feet. The head would be thrown from side to side so swiftly that the features would be blotted out and the hair made to snap. When the body was affected, the sufferer was hurled over hindrances that came in his way, and finally dashed to the ground to bounce about like a ball . . ." [13] The rather gleeful description of one of the frontier exhorters assures us that: "I have seen more than 500 persons jerking at one time in my large congregations. Most usually persons taken with the jerks, to obtain relief as they said, would rise up

[12] McMaster, *op. cit.,* II, p. 580. The use of the term "slain" may have come from the description of one such scene by a prominent frontier church leader quoted in Clark, *op. cit.,* p. 116: "Many, very many fell down as men slain in battle and continued for hours together in an apparently breathless state."

[13] McMaster, *loc. cit.*

and dance. Some would run, but could not get away; some would resist, on such the jerks were generally very severe . . . To see those proud young gentlemen and ladies, dressed in their silks, jewelry and prunella from top to toe, take the jerks would often excite my risibilities. The first jerk or so, you would see their fine bonnets, caps and combs fly; and so sudden would be the jerking of the head that their long loose hair would crack almost as loud as a waggoner's whip." [14]

McMaster thus describes a third example of common occurrence: "During the most earnest preaching and exhorting, even sincere professors of religion, would, on a sudden, burst into loud laughter; others, unable to resist, would follow, and soon the assembled multitude would join in. This was the "Holy Laugh," and became, after 1803, a recognized part of worship." [15] Another type of hysteria was the "gift of tongues," which was bestowed by the Holy Spirit, these deluded frontiersmen believed, when some emotionally overwrought unfortunate lost control of his organs of speech and mouthed a flood of unintelligible gibberish.

Possibly the most repugnant of these "gifts of the Holy Spirit" was "the barks" and the subsequent "treeing the devil." "From the nerves and muscles the disorder passed to the mind. Men dreamed dreams and saw visions, nay, fancied themselves dogs, went down on all fours, and barked until they grew hoarse. It was no uncommon sight

[14] Cartwright, *op. cit.*, pp. 48-49.
[15] McMaster, *loc. cit.*

to behold numbers of them gathered about a tree, barking, yelping, "treeing the devil." [16]

Nor was this mass hysteria the only evil consequence of the abandonment of reason in the emotional orgies of the revival. The unrestrained surrender to the passions occasionally produced lasting insanity or death among the afflicted persons.[17] The jettisoning of reason led also to other abuses scarcely in conformity with the avowed purpose of the revivals to "convert" the people from their sins.[18]

Waves of revivalism passed over the frontier during the course of half a century. As the middle of the 19th Century approached, the revivals and camp meetings became less frequent, extreme examples of mass hysteria became less

[16] McMaster, *loc. cit.* For further details of this hysteria, cf. *inter alios,* Loud, *op. cit.,* p. 112 ff.; Tyler, Alice F., *Freedom's Ferment,* p. 35 ff.; and Davenport, Frederick M., *Primitive Traits in Religious Revivals,* p. 60 ff.

[17] Rowe, *op. cit.,* p. 66: "Men and women rolled on the ground, foamed at the mouth, jerked their heads, arms and legs, or even went mad with fear." Cf. Clark, *op. cit.,* p. 114.

[18] Bates, *op. cit.,* p. 337 ff.; Davenport, *op. cit.,* p. 81 ff. Since the revival was the greatest single factor in the spread of Evangelical Protestantism in America, both in the period of the Great Awakening and throughout the first half of the 19th Century, Protestant authors very understandably do not like to dwell on the mass hysteria and other repugnant consequences arising from the very nature of the revival. The impression that the reader obtains from such volumes as the *History of American Revivals* by Frank G. Beardsley is that the camp meetings were conducted with the decorum and restraint of a minuet.

Sweet, *Story,* p. 8, attempts a half-hearted defense of frontier revivalism: "But whatever may be said in criticism of frontier revivalism, this much must be said in its behalf: it was perhaps the only method by which the frontier could receive any of the benefits of Christianity, warped though it often was almost beyond recognition." A critic might point out that Sweet's statement is a rather open application of the principle that the end justifies the means.

common, the numbers of new church members garnered by the revival method for organized religion became fewer. Some districts of the borderlands had been evangelized so often that revivalism could no longer stir the jaded emotions of the populace. A prominent frontier exhorter reported lamentable conditions prevailing in the 1840's in some of these "burnt-over" localities, "so blistered by constant revival flame that no sprout, no blade of spiritual life could be caused to grow; only the apples of Sodom flourished in the form of religious ignorance, intolerance, a boasted sinlessness and a tendency to free love . . ."[19]

The reaction of the frontier environment on Christianity had large consequences for American Protestantism. One of the most notable was the rise of new sects. Many of these new churches were schisms, for "between 1790 and 1830 substantially every older denomination had experienced a schism due to the fact that the main body could not keep up with the more radical spirit of the frontier."[20] Eastern congregations viewed with disfavor the camp meeting excesses of their Western co-religionists, and the borderland congregations held in disdain the middle-class respectability of seaboard Christianity; frequently the separation of the sects followed these sectional lines. As, when the frontier advanced, the original pioneers gave way to middle-class farmers and tradesmen, as towns, schools, industry and communications developed, the Evangelical sects of the West began their evolution into sects of the bourgeoisie.

[19] Quoted in Neve, *op. cit.,* p. 398.
[20] Douglass, *op. cit.,* p. 33.

This trend towards religious respectability was opposed by many members who desired the continuance of frontier religion. Often these conflicting trends occasioned the rise of new sects.

The Disciples of Christ, one of the largest of the Evangelical sects, arose through the amalgamation of some of these Western schisms. This new denomination sought to unite all Protestants in a single creedless church, an aim which, paradoxically enough, has served rather to multiply sects in Protestantism.[21] The Disciples were organized by Alexander Campbell, a Presbyterian minister who, with a group of Presbyterian followers, sought a purer faith in the Baptist communion about 1813. Finding the Baptist church not in conformity with his ideals, Campbell initiated a reform movement which found adherents in many mid-Western Baptist congregations. The "Reformers" gradually established their own congregations, separated from the Baptist communion, assumed the "creedless" name of Disciples of Christ, and united to themselves groups from other sects undergoing a similar process of evolution. Some of the Reformers, however, remained apart from the Disciples to cast in their lot with the Christian Church (or

[21] Already extant in the United States were the Moravian Brethren, known also as the *Unitas Fratrum,* a sect which strove for the same end but which succeeded only in producing at least two schisms. This aim of unity reached perhaps the ultimate frustration in the sect of the Plymouth Brethren, or Darbyites, a minor group founded for the express purpose of supplying a basis on which all Protestant denominations could unite. The net result was that this minuscule group broke into eight almost indiscernible but mutually opposed sects. Even the Protestant proclivity to find a name for the smallest sect was defeated by the Darbyites. Their sects are simply labeled from Group I to Group VIII.

the Churches of Christ); many Methodists formed their own Methodist Protestant Church.[22]

In the number and strange tenets of many small frontier sects, even fissiparous Protestantism seems to have exceeded itself. The borderlands accepted without criticism and applied in the most unexpected fashion a popular axiom of the times "to speak where the Bible speaks; to be silent where the Bible is silent." Opposition to "unscriptural" devices was raised to the level of a dogma. Since Sunday Schools, organs and other musical instruments in divine services, missionary societies and boards, and education for the clergy are not mentioned in Holy Writ, proposals for the adoption of such advances by the denominations met with a storm of opposition. These disputes led to many "anti" schisms, particularly among the Baptists, whose "anti" elements have been labeled "Hard Shell" or "Landmarker." The application of the Biblical axiom reached its apogee among the Pilgrims, a small group who could find no Biblical sanction for bathing.

Moral as well as Biblical questions produced several frontier schisms. Schisms over moral problems aided the Mennonites in achieving the undesired distinction of being the most divided small denomination in America. In 1847 the General Conference of Mennonites appeared

[22] The title "Church of Christ" or "Churches of Christ" has been assumed by a very large number of Protestant sects, particularly among the innumerable groups of the "Holiness" type founded at the close of the 19th Century. The Churches of Christ mentioned here should not be confused with a similar and contemporaneous movement in New England which adopted the same name. Some of these churches merged with the Congregational Church in 1931. Nor should this Church of Christ be confused with a 20th Century schism from the Disciples of Christ.

as the result of a dispute over the cut of a minister's coat. In 1850 the Conservative Amish Mennonites emerged as a distinct sect as the outcome of an argument whether baptism should be administered indoors in still water, or outdoors in running water.[23] The knotty problem whether or not it was permissible for a man to conceal his knowledge of the hiding place of his children from marauding Indians if they put the question to him divided one Baptist group into "Lying" and "Truthful" Baptists.

Even more peculiar sects appeared. The extant "Two-Seed-in-the-Spirit Predestinarian Baptists" revivified Manichaeanism. This minuscule sect teaches that man's eternal destiny is determined by the "seed" with which he is born. If a man is fortunate enough to arrive in this world with a "good" seed, his eternal happiness in heaven has been assured; his fate is quite otherwise if he faces life with a "bad" seed. Another strange group were the Followers of Christ. This antinomian group, founded by a "prophet" noted for his austerity (proven by the fact that he had not changed his clothes in seven years), rejected the use of surnames, forbade marriage and practised promiscuous cohabitation.

Western New York, so often evangelized that it was known as the "burnt-over district" par excellence, produced the strangest and the most important galaxy of the new religious aberrations. Here was located the notorious Oneida Community. This famed group of religious communists, founded by the antinomian John Humphrey

[23] Clark, *op. cit.,* pp. 228, 235. The author, p. 227, mentions the rise of the Reformed Mennonites in 1812 after a dispute over a horse trade.

Noyes, was noted chiefly for the practise of "plural marriage"; every man in the organization was the husband of each and every woman in the community.[24] In Western New York the spirits of the Fox Sisters first knocked their way to fame.[25] Soon spiritualism was to count its congregations by the thousands and its believers by the hundreds of thousands.[26]

Of greater import in the history of American Protestantism was the emergence in that same "burnt-over district" of the Church of Jesus Christ of the Latter-Day Saints, the Mormons of Joseph Smith.

Smith claimed to be a visionary and a prophet to whom had been given a new revelation. This manifestation of God to man, he declared, was contained in the Book of Mormon, a volume written on gold plates and discovered to Joseph by an angel. Since the manuscript was composed in a language and a script unknown to philologists, the angel thoughtfully provided Smith with two pieces of stone, the "Urim and Thummin," which, when placed in his eyes, enabled him to translate the famous Book into English strangely reminiscent of the King James Version. Although amanuenses had copied down Smith's translation, Smith, by dictating from behind a curtain, had deprived them of the opportunity to see the precious golden volume. When Smith's critics challenged him to

[24] Cf. Bates, *op. cit.,* p. 390 ff.; Tyler, *op. cit.,* p. 184 ff.

[25] Tyler, *op. cit.,* p. 82 ff.

[26] Lyon, *op. cit.,* p. 231; Weigle, *op. cit.,* p. 172; Sweet, *Story,* p. 404. For details on spiritualism, cf. the two volumes of Ferguson, Charles W., *The Confusion of Tongues,* p. 15 ff., and *New Books of Revelations,* p. 15 ff. On recent spiritualism, see Atkins, Gaius G., *Modern Religious Cults and Movements,* p. 284 ff.

produce the book, it had, he regretfully informed his inquisitors, been removed by the angel. But he provided the sworn testimony of three men who had seen the marvelous volume. Nor was the sturdy faith of the early Mormons shaken when all three "witnesses" later recanted their belief in Mormonism.[27]

Preaching his new Gospel, Smith found little difficulty in collecting a number of followers in the "burnt-over" district. But since his past had been none too Puritan and since unconverted New Yorkers insisted on making difficulties for his flock, he led his adherents to greener pastures in the West, where his apostles had gathered numerous other sheep. Dissensions within the fold and troubles with non-Mormons—especially after rumors of polygamy had been bruited about—made several western states too hot for the new sect.[28] Smith was finally killed by an irate mob in a Missouri jail.

On the news of its leader's death, the sect broke into a number of schisms. The majority, however, were reorganized under the leadership of Brigham Young and migrated to Utah where they established the "State of Deseret." Their desire to settle outside the reach of the persecuting "Gentiles" of the United States, however, was soon brought to naught by the American acquisition of their new home

[27] Werner, *op. cit.*, p. 45. Some wags once offered Smith several plates of brass on which they had scratched meaningless lines. Smith pronounced the plates to be repositories of authentic revelations and with the help of Urim and Thummin translated the bogus writing into a paean of praise of Mormonism's prophet. Cf. Loud, *op. cit.*, p. 147 f.

[28] That the rumor was not without foundation is indicated by the fact that Smith himself had at least twenty-eight wives. Werner, *op. cit.*, p. 146.

as a consequence of the Mexican War. In Utah the Mormons openly utilized the "revelation" enjoining the practise of polygamy; many of the leaders showed the way by acquiring notable harems.[29] It was not until the close of the 19th Century that, under pressure from the Federal government, the elders of the sect announced a new revelation suspending the practise of polygamy among the Saints.

Orthodox Christians continued to view the sect with suspicion, not only for its polygamy, but for its incipient polytheism. For the Mormons affirmed that "God was himself once as we are now, and is an exalted man." [30] They declared that spirits, which by some paradox are nothing more than refined matter, are conceived by the wives of polygamous gods and inserted in human bodies as the first step in their evolution to godhood.[31] Due to these early polygamous and later polytheistic inclinations, it is questionable whether the Latter-Day Saints can be considered Christian, even in the widest sense of that much abused word.

A few years after the exodus of Joseph Smith and his Mormons, the East hailed another "prophet." Through the years of the Thirties, the New England Baptist William Miller journeyed about predicting the imminent advent of the millennium. Within a short time, remarkably large numbers of the lower economic classes had accepted the prophet and his preaching of the imminent Parousia.[32]

---

[29] Cf. Werner, *op. cit.,* pp. 325, 340.

[30] Quoted in Neve, *op. cit.,* p. 588.

[31] *Ibid;* Weigle, *op. cit.,* p. 245.

[32] Channing, *op. cit.,* V, p. 234: "The number of his followers was extraordinary—more than extraordinary . . . ." Tyler, *op. cit.,* p. 70 ff.

When, on the first day Miller had selected as the last day, the heavens and the earth continued undisturbed in their orbits, the Millerites, undisturbed, chose another doomsday. When this second day passed without the occurrence of the universal catastrophe, Miller, undaunted, continued his preaching of imminent doom, but appointed no third day of final judgment.

On the appointed days, however, large numbers of willing dupes gave remarkable demonstrations of their faith in the prophet.[33] In preparation for the day of doom, many had sold all they had and given to the poor; farmers declined to plant crops; tradesmen had discharged their employes and closed down their businesses. On the day of destiny, throngs of the faithful crowded their churches, or climbed to tops of hills. Stories are recounted of Millerites who had thoughtfully prepared their celestial clothing and appeared on the great day in flowing white robes; one young lady, it is told, firmly strapped herself to a trunk containing her best apparel in her determination to be well dressed amid the angelic choirs.[34]

Though the prophet proved false, many clung to the millennial hopes he had stirred. Congregations of Millerites persisted and were joined by groups from other sects which had been permeated by Millerite millennialism. These deluded people organized the Seventh Day Adventists and the other sects of the Adventist group.

Revivalism, millennialism and the borderland schisms

[33] Loud, *op. cit.*, p. 177, declares that more than 40,000 had made their preparations for the last day.

[34] Sears, Clara E., *Days of Delusion*, p. 160 ff., recounts many stories of the days of doom.

were but a few factors of the influence of the frontier on American Protestantism. At the end of the frontier, the Evangelical sects had become the largest Protestant denominations in America. It is estimated that during the first half of the 19th Century the Baptists increased their church membership from 100,000 to 800,000, and the Methodists registered a tremendous increase from 65,000 to 1,250,000.[35] It must be noted, however, that this tremendous increase on the frontier of Evangelical church membership—for other Evangelical sects probably registered comparable gains—was derived, partially at least, from the membership of the older Protestant denominations. For the frontiersmen were not pagans, but Christians who had left the churches behind. The Protestant sects best suited to the environment of the borderlands had in the new West made the major efforts for the evangelization of the pioneers and reaped the major gains in new church membership.

The American policy of separation of Church and State had already forced on the American people the practise of voluntary contributions for the support of their ecclesiastical institutions. Since the financial needs of the frontier evangelization had to be and were met by the people themselves, the policy of voluntary support of religion was thereby more strongly established. The missionary societies and boards which were created to publicize and collect funds for the work of Western evangelization facilitated the transition to the work of foreign missions. While the first American Protestant foreign missioners did not invade pagan lands until the 19th Century, by the end of that

[35] Channing, *op. cit.*, V, p. 221.

century American Protestantism was well on its way to unchallenged preeminence in the field of Protestant foreign missions.

The frontier assisted the growth of a movement towards the reunion of the Protestant sects, a trend which was to reach major proportions in the 20th Century. Frontier Christianity produced several churches explicitly aimed at the coalescence of Protestant denominations into one church, and by its singular lack of interest in dogma minimized the theological differences separating the sects. The sects gained a practical appreciation of the expediency of cooperation through interdenominational mission boards and conferences and the joint conduct of revivals by ministers of several denominations. Conversely, however, the new frontier sects, the innumerable frontier schisms and the fierce denominational rivalry in the recruitment of frontier church members strengthened the grip of denominationalism on American Protestantism.

The conservative Eastern reaction to the excesses of the frontier revivals and camp meetings gave impetus to the growth of the liberal Protestant theology in the bourgeois sects of the seaboard towns. While the harsh doctrine of infant damnation was questioned and rejected by humane Protestants of all denominations, the dogma of the "conversion," due to the Western emotional orgies, gained disrepute even among the more cultured members of Eastern Evangelical denominations. While the advance of the liberal theology did not, generally speaking, cause schisms within the denominations, several new liberal sects made their appearance. The Universalists were a recognized denomination early in the 19th Century, and Unitarian schismatics from Congregationalism established their own independent religious organization in 1825.

The religious chasm between East and West was widened and deepened by the increasing identification of the sects with economic and social classes, and even with the political parties. Congregationalists and Episcopalians, for example, were almost exclusively members of the middle and upper-classes, liberal in theology, conservative in politics. To be a Congregationalist was to be a Federalist and a Whig; conversion to the Methodists or Baptists was equivalent to a declaration of adhesion to the principles of the Democratic Republicans.[36] Thus sectionalism, political principles and the class system united to widen the breaches in Protestantism.

While Evangelical Protestantism was gathering new strength in the borderlands, the Catholic Church was laying the groundwork for its tremendous future expansion by its labors in the poorer districts of the Eastern cities.

The great demands of the East made impossible any major Catholic efforts for the evangelization of the Western frontier. The Catholic Church had neither the priests nor the financial support necessary for that task. Throughout the 19th Century the Catholic Americans were notoriously poor, and the Church was forced to devote its slender resources to the enormous task of erecting the necessary churches and schools in centers where Catholics were

---

[36] Douglass, *op. cit.*, p. 32, quotes a writer on the times: "Every convert to Methodism in those times became a Republican, if he was not one before."

numerous. Nor could the Catholic Church flood the borderlands with evangelists by a practise of elevating illiterate
exhorters to her sacred ministry. Indeed, the rigorous educational requirements of the Church for promotion to the
priesthood brought about a perennial shortage of priests
even in the East. For although the ranks of the Catholic
clergy were continually augmented by volunteers from
Europe and although increasingly numerous aspirants for
the priesthood entered the growing number of American
seminaries, the Catholic clergy were never, throughout the
19th Century, sufficiently numerous to care for the expanding Church in the United States.

Nevertheless, the frontier was neither forgotten nor
ignored. When the See of Baltimore was elevated, in 1808,
to the status of an archdiocese, one of the suffragan bishops
was established in the borderlands of the West. Since the
priests of this Western diocese were few in number, their
energies perforce were spent not in evangelization but in
the spiritual care of their small but very scattered flocks;
their travels were as long and as arduous as the journeys of
the Methodist circuit riders. While the Church gained comparatively few new members on the borderlands, the early
labors of these pioneer priests prepared the ground for
the future expansion of the Catholic Church in the West.

On the chosen frontier of the Church, the poorer districts
of the Eastern towns and cities, Catholicism expanded tre-
mendously. Each decade of the 19th Century to the Civil
War saw the numbers of Catholics advance by almost
geometrical progression. While in 1800 American Catholics
were about 50,000 in number, the Church had almost

200,000 communicants in the United States in 1820, and by 1840 this number had grown to over 650,000.[37] In the latter year the See of Baltimore had been joined by fifteen other dioceses, and the Catholic Church had become, in point of church membership, one of the five largest American churches.

This great increase of Catholic church membership was due to immigration. It is estimated that between 1820 and 1865, 1,880,000 Irish and 1,545,000 German immigrants, together with 750,000 English and large numbers of other nationalities had entered the United States.[38] While substantial numbers of the Germans were Catholic, the great majority of the Irish were unquestionably members of the Catholic Church.[39]

The advent of the immigrants provided a searching test of the ability of Catholicism to retain the allegiance of its European members in a strange and frequently hostile environment. The prime task of Catholicism was to keep the immigrants in one Church amidst the welter of sects and schisms which American conditions had occasioned in Protestantism. In the attainment of this primary end the Catholic Church was eminently successful. While the majority of the numerous Protestant immigrants either sloughed off their connections with organized Christianity or established new sects to supply their particular religious

---

[37] Shaughnessy, *op. cit.,* p. 189.

[38] Latourette, *op. cit.,* IV, p. 225.

[39] The statement of Sweet, *Story,* p. 390, that the Irish were "a hundred percent Roman Catholic" is an exaggeration. Cf. Shaughnessy, *op. cit.,* p. 108 ff., for a study of the number of Catholics among the Irish immigrants.

needs, "in the main, however, the Catholic Church, while winning comparatively few who were not traditionally of its Faith, seems to have retained the allegiance of the large majority of the immigrants who in Europe had been in its fold." [40]

From Europe together with the immigrants came priests and financial aid to assist the building of the new Church. A considerable number of the 500 priests attending the 650,000 American Catholics in 1840 had been born in Europe and educated in Catholic seminaries abroad. The contributions of several European organizations, notably the Society for the Propagation of the Faith, the *Ludwigsmissionsverein* and the Leopoldine Association, eased the financial burden of the Church in America. [41]

Yet the main burden of building the material structure of the Church in the United States was assumed by the American Catholics. In this necessary work, poverty-stricken immigrants played an heroic role. Speaking of their sacrifices, Latourette writes: "The majority contributed out of their poverty. It is striking evidence of their religious conviction and of the fashion in which their Faith had become an integral part of their lives, that, coming as most of them did, from lands in which the Roman Catholic Church had state support . . . they voluntarily gave out of their small incomes." [42]

From the families of the immigrants came also a large

[40] Latourette, *op. cit.*, IV, p. 255. This statement is applied by the author to the whole course of United States history.

[41] Cf. Corrigan, Raymond, *The Church and the Nineteenth Century*, pp. 81-93.

[42] Latourette, *op. cit.*, IV, p. 247.

and ever increasing proportion of the Catholic clergy. While many of these aspirants to the priesthood received their theological training in Europe, the greater number were educated in seminaries in the United States. The first major American seminary was opened in 1791; by 1840 it had been joined by several other institutions engaged in the same work.

While the Catholic Church was in process of construction, it undoubtedly suffered some leakage in church membership. The inadequate number of priests, churches and schools, the anti-Catholic atmosphere and tradition of the United States, religious indifferentism and other factors all took their toll. It is impossible to determine the extent of the leakage; but it is clear that no such alarming apostasies as had occurred in the colonial period took place. Save for the apostasy of some newly-freed Negroes after the Civil War and a minuscule schism of some Slav congregations at the end of the century, the losses suffered by the Catholic Church were the defections of individuals, not groups. No mass movement out of the Catholic Church in America can be discerned throughout the whole course of the 19th Century.[43]

Yet the Catholic Church, while it solved the enormous problems posed by the presence of the immigrants, was not impervious to the influence of the American environment. The religious principles and the nationalistic divisions of the dominant Protestant majority in the United States could not but exercise a profound influence on early

[43] On this Negro leakage, cf. Gillard, John T., *The Catholic Church and the American Negro*, p. 258.

Catholics. This influence was manifested throughout the first half of the 19th Century by sporadic but explosive outbursts of "trustee troubles" which required strong disciplinary action on the part of the Catholic hierarchy.[44]

The "trustee troubles," which later were intensified by the introduction of nationalistic antipathies, originated in attempts by Catholic laymen to gain permanent control of their local congregations and were generally precipitated by unworthy priests.[45] In the opening decades of the 19th Century Catholic parish property, in accordance with the provisions of state legislation, was vested, following the usual practise of the Protestant denominations, in laymen chosen by the local congregation. This lay control of church property proved a permanent cause of conflict.[46] On many occasions the lay trustees exceeded the limitations of their proper powers by claiming the right of patronage which Protestant trustees exercised over the churches in their control.[47] The conflicts between the Hierarchy and the

[44] Trusteemania still existed in the Sixties. Possibly the first outbreak occurred among German Catholics as early as 1786. Cf. O'Gorman, op. cit., p. 279. A contemporary account will be found in Griffin, Martin I. J. (ed), Documents relating to the History of the Catholic Church in the U.S., I, p. 143 f.

[45] Guilday, England, I, p. 9: "In the final analysis of each of the trustee troubles . . . the cause was always a priest who, wishing to escape the jurisdiction of the bishop or to thwart just punishment for unbecoming or scandalous conduct, sided with the troublesome trustees and augmented the complexity of the problem at issue with the subtler and more dangerous one of lay patronage."

[46] Dignan, Patrick J., Legal Incorporation of Catholic Church Property, p. 96: "But racial antagonism, however dangerous it proved in such places as New York, Charleston and Norfolk, was accidental to the spirit of rebellion which seemed to grow out of the trustee system . . ."

[47] Cf. Mode, op. cit., p. 451, for an interesting document in which lay trustees openly claimed the right of patronage.

trustees were usually precipitated when, for just cause, a bishop attempted to withdraw a contumacious or scandalous priest from his post over the objections of the lay trustees and the refusal of the priest.[48]

In several cases the trustees proved obdurate and the priest disobedient for two or three years. In a number of instances, Catholic congregations went into open schism.[49] Sometimes these small schisms endured for several years, with the contumacious priests suspended, the trustees excommunicated, and the parish churches under interdict. In every case, however, the schism was finally healed, and the turbulent congregations, though not without some permanent individual defections, reduced to their proper obedience.

In the earlier decades of the 19th Century "trusteemania" was rendered more acute by the additional complication of nationalism. Many *émigré* clerics, driven to America by the French Revolution, had been elevated to bishoprics in the United States. As more and more French bishops were appointed—in 1817 all the bishops in the United States, save one, were Frenchmen—Irish Catholics suspected a French plot to dominate the Church in America. When, then, French prelates sent French priests to supersede in Irish parishes priests of Irish blood, the result was trouble.

[48] Bayley, James R., *History of the Catholic Church on the Island of N.Y.*, p. 65: "The trustee system had not been behind in its early promise, and (by 1815) trustees of churches had become so accustomed to have everything their own way, that they were not disposed to allow even the interference of a bishop."

[49] For an account of the most notorious of these ephemeral schisms, cf. Tourcher, Francis E., *The Hogan Schism.*

As the unedifying conflict between rebellious trustees and the Hierarchy proceeded, "all the old causes of the quarrel . . . were forgotten in the larger question of race against race." [50] Irish trustees appealed to Rome over their bishops' heads, and some bolder spirits among them contemplated the establishment of an "Independent Catholick Church."[51] Nor was the acrimony entirely from the Irish. Archbishop Marechal, of Baltimore, spoke of *"la canaille irlandaise"* and wrote on the appointment of some Irish bishops to American sees: *"Je n'ai que des nouvelles disastreuses à vous donner. La Propaganda a rejeté les missionaires éprouvés que moi et mes suffragants lui avaient recommendés. Elle leur a préferé des prêtres irlandais."* [52] Nevertheless, the appointment of Irish bishops and the diminution of French representation in the American Hierarchy by the death or transfer of the *émigré* bishops brought the disedifying racial quarrel to a natural and unlamented end. By the end of the fourth decade of the 19th Century, the culmination of the French-Irish conflict was passed, and the final eradication of trusteemania was assured.

The final victory of the Hierarchy was guaranteed by the measures formulated against trusteeism by the American bishops convened in the First Provincial Council of Baltimore in 1829. From the issuance of the Council's decrees may be dated the decline of the trustee troubles. The legislation of the initial Council was reaffirmed in several

[50] Guilday, *Trusteeism,* p. 73; Shearer, *op. cit.,* p. 107 ff.; p. 118 ff.
[51] Guilday, *England,* I, p. 262 ff.
[52] Guilday, *Trusteeism,* p. 60. Cf. Dignan, *op. cit.,* pp. 96-97.

subsequent Provincial Councils, and was extended to the whole Church in America by the First Plenary Council of Baltimore in 1852. While outbursts of trustee trouble occurred sporadically for at least another decade, the virus of trusteemania had been effectively isolated and the remedies suggested by the Conciliar legislation proved quickly effective.

Though trusteemania and the French-Irish quarrel had been both disheartening and extremely dangerous, the successful solution of these problems by the Catholic Church underlined an important aspect of the history of Christianity in the United States. Though new breaches in Protestantism were opened by untrammeled nationalism and uncontrolled democracy, the Catholic Church proved that it could unite in an undivided Church the most disparate nationalities the melting-pot of America could offer.

CHAPTER VI

NO POPERY

THE history of bigotry is a long, bloody and dishonorable record. To that sad story the United States has contributed a disheartening chapter. In America both religion and race have been the objects of the bigots' hate. But while members of many nationalities have experienced racial discriminations, the history of religious bigotry in the United States is almost exclusively a record of anti-Catholicism. For while colonial Americans had persecuted not only Catholics but dissenting Protestants, opposition to Evangelical Protestantism had abated long before the adoption of the Federal Constitution.

Anti-Catholicism, however, remained.[1] While the fearful hatred of the Catholic Church has been a permanent factor in the history of our nation, anti-Catholicism reached its acme of influence and virulence in the decades immediately preceding the Civil War. "What the capitalist was to Lenin

---

[1] Strangely enough, the literature on anti-Catholicism has been written almost exclusively by non-Catholics. Some have written in extremely bitter vein, e.g., Dieffenbach, Albert C., *Religious Liberty: The Great American Illusion.* On the bigotry of the Know Nothing era, cf., besides the works cited in the subsequent notes, Myers, Gustavus, *History of Bigotry in the U.S.*, p. 140 ff.; Maury, Reuben, *The Wars of the Godly*, p. 53 ff.; and Clinchy, Everett R., *All in the Name of God*, p. 69 ff.

in 1917 and the Jew to Hitler in 1935, the Catholic was
to the American democrat in the middle of the 19th Century. The ogre of American democracy was the Scarlet
Lady of Babylon. The shadow of the Reformation (sic)
still lay across America." [2]

The swift growth of the Catholic Church had aroused
the alarms of the bigots. During the decade of the Forties
the number of Catholic faithful had mounted from 663,000
to 1,600,000 while by the middle of the subsequent decade
the Catholic Church had over 2,000,000 adherents in the
United States.[3] Within a score of years the Catholic Church
had grown from a minor denomination to one of the four
largest religious groups in the nation.

Other factors besides the fear of Catholic numbers in-
flamed the hatred of the bigots. While European immigration had swelled the ranks of the Catholic Church in
America, the influx of poverty-stricken immigrants had
also brought about an increase in pauperism, crime and
intemperance. These lamentable developments, most noticeable in the poorer districts of the larger cities and towns,
were immediately laid to the presence of the numerous
Catholics in the same districts. The laboring classes saw in
the immigrants competitors for employment, and the
middle and upper-classes feared the political potentialities
of these new citizens.[4]

While the anti-Catholic propaganda of the Protestant
sects had never ceased, by the end of the Thirties it had

[2] Gabriel, Ralph H., *Course of American Democratic Thought,* p. 52.

[3] Shaughnessy, *op. cit.,* p. 189.

[4] For a discussion of the causes of Nativism, cf. Guilday, *England,* II,
p. 215 ff.

shown a marked increase in volume and intensification in violence. The Bible, tract, home and foreign missionary societies, as well as the Protestant pulpits, took up the "No Popery" cry. "Anti-Catholicism became a nation-wide movement." [5]

Bigotry has never shown nicety in its choice of weapons. In this intensified propaganda, the anti-Catholics, without regard for the truth, twisted the Catholic position in civil and religious matters to afford a handle for hate. Thus the struggle of the American Catholic Hierarchy against the abuses of trusteeism was pilloried as an attack on American democracy. Catholics objected to the reading to their children in the public schools of the Protestant King James Version of the Bible and disliked the practise of many teachers who disseminated the assumption that, since all churches were liable to error in Biblical interpretation, each individual should interpret Holy Writ for himself. When Catholics dared openly to voice their complaints, the bigots distorted the Catholic objections into an obscurantist Catholic attack on the inspired Word of God.

To the tocsin calls of ecclesiastics was added the clamor of a new weapon of propaganda, the religious periodical press. Most of the Protestant newspapers and magazines devoted regular sections of their issues to attacks on Catholicism. Several papers were established for the express purpose of combating the Catholic menace and exposing the Papal plots. Anything anti-Catholic was assured a place in their columns. John Hughes, later Catholic Archbishop of New York, sent to one of the earliest of these sheets, *The*

[5] Gabriel, *op. cit.,* p. 53.

Protestant, a contribution which he considered manifestly absurd. When the credulous editors published the incredible manuscript, Hughes sent them a series of anonymous papers, each more foolish than the preceding; all promptly appeared in print. Discovering no end to the gullibility of bigots, Hughes had finally to expose himself. Nor were magazines and newspapers of this type the only products of the bigot press. Floods of anti-Catholic broadsheets, pamphlets and books inundated the country.

These verbal attacks led ultimately and inevitably to violence. With the Thirties, rioting began. St. Mary's Catholic Church in New York City was burned by the bigots in 1831. In 1834, following a sermon exposing an alleged Popish plot to seize the Mississippi Valley, a crowd of Boston hoodlums attacked, pillaged and burned a Charlestown convent.[6]

Violence, as usual, begat violence. While the spirit of the attack on Catholicism was intensified by rioting and arson, the flood of propaganda was swelled by a new and muddy stream of pornography. The salacious lectures of apostate priests and of women posing as "ex-nuns" were attended by crowds whose expectations were not disappointed.

The most notorious of these "ex-nuns," a woman self-styled "Maria Monk," published the *Awful Disclosures,* the most infamous and the best selling of the pornographic books. Published in 1836, the volume sold about 300,000 copies before the Civil War. While it was true, as the book

---

[6] Shea, *op. cit.,* III, p. 473 ff., describes this famous incident; he writes, p. 478: "The mob did not spare even the graves of the dead (nuns). The coffins were torn open and the bodies exposed."

asserted, that Maria Monk had been in a convent, she had scarcely been there as a nun. The convent was a refuge for wayward girls, from which Maria, who had been committed there, managed to escape. Her life thereafter was not above reproach. She seized the opportunity presented by her first illegitimate offspring by attributing its fatherhood to a priest. A later fatherless baby, however, she did not attempt to lay to the charge of the Catholic clergy. Despite Maria's exposure as a liar and a fraud by her own mother, and despite her later career of drunkenness, felony and promiscuity, her book became standard reading for the period and was accepted by thousands as a true history.[7]

During the decade of the Forties further fuel was added to the flames of bigotry by the school question. While the issue was debated on a nation-wide scale, the most important contest was waged in New York City. There, strangely enough, the dispute was occasioned not by the Catholics but by the Baptists.

The school funds of New York City were distributed, in accordance with the provisions of a state law passed in 1812, to private and parochial as well as public schools. The city's system of public schools was under the supervision of a private educational corporation, the Free School Society, later known as the Public School Society. Control evidently led to greed, for subsequently the Public School Society manifested a desire to acquire all the funds assigned to education.[8] Its campaign for the monopoly of these

[7] Cf. Billington, Ray A., *The Protestant Crusade*, p. 99 ff., for an account of Maria Monk and her associates.

[8] Gabel, Richard J., *Public Funds for Church and Private Schools,* p. 354.

public funds was initiated when, in 1822, it attacked the application of the Baptist Bethel Church for public aid for its parochial school. The petition of the Baptists was supported by the Methodist, Episcopal, Dutch Reformed and Catholic Churches, which all desired continued state grants in aid of their parochial educational institutions. The disputants eventually carried their debate to the New York courts, which sustained the position of the Public School Society.

The judicial decision, however, did not end the matter. The Catholics continued to press their campaign for state aid to the parochial schools and to urge their objections against the King James Version in the public schools. The Public School Society, however, soon found that powerful and unscrupulous allies had come to its aid. The bigots rushed in to battle against this new Catholic attack on American liberties. "The Protestant clergy and many sectarian journals were prominent in the campaign of vilification of Catholic principles and practises, and in the school controversy more space was devoted to repeating ancient calumnies and describing the imminent peril of 'papal domination,' particularly of the mid-West, than to the question at issue." [9]

When, in 1842, the Catholics of New York, together with one Jewish synagogue and one Scotch Presbyterian congregation, again appealed to state officials for public funds for their schools, their petition was foredoomed to failure. It is interesting to note that their petition was opposed not only by the Public School Society, but "by some churches,

[9] *Ibid*, p. 295 n.

Methodist, Baptist, Dutch Reformed and Reformed Presbyterians." [10] The radical change of front within twenty years by these Protestant denominations evidently was caused by some powerful influences. Gabel asserts that: "The greatest unifying factor for 'non-sectarian' public education turned out to be the large influx of Catholic immigrants . . ." [11]

Despite this reverse, however, the Catholics were more successful in their campaign against the anti-Catholic teaching in the schools of the Public School Society. When the bigotry in the Public School Society's textbooks was exposed by Archbishop Hughes in an "Address of the Roman Catholics," the Society admitted the justice of the charge and undertook an expurgation of the offending books.[12] Finally, the legislature of New York State terminated the apparently interminable quarrel by legislating the Public School Society out of existence in 1842.

While the Catholics gained by this legislative action, inasmuch as public education was removed from the arbitrary control of a private corporation which was opposed to religious education and tainted with bigotry, the school dispute, though necessary, was generally speaking calamitous. Although the Catholic Church continued the construction of its system of parochial schools and the Catholic faithful assumed the burden of a double tax for the education of their children, the Protestant denominations, due partly at least to antipathy to Catholicism, allowed them-

[10] *Ibid*, p. 357.
[11] *Ibid*, p. 700.
[12] Shea, *op. cit.*, IV, pp. 526-527, prints the main points of this address.

selves to be identified as partisans of the principle of "non-sectarian" public education.[13]

While the school question was being disputed in the press, the courts and the legislatures, the anti-Catholic debate continued in the streets. Throughout the early years of the Forties, the tempo of riots, arson and bloodshed mounted towards a climax. The increasing attacks on Catholic churches, convents and schools led to the posting of armed Catholic volunteers about church property. In several instances, however, Catholic church buildings were destroyed. Nor were the dwellings of Catholics spared; frequent torches were applied to the homes of the Irish and other Catholic immigrants. The attitude of the Irish, never irenic, did not make for peace. Not only did they defend their churches and homes vigorously, but in some instances they assumed the role of aggressors. On occasion, groups of belligerent Irishmen stopped passers-by in the open streets, asked their religious affiliation, and gave the answer the reception they believed it deserved.

The Philadelphia riots in 1844 supplied a climax to this early period of rioting, when for three days the City of Brotherly Love was a battleground. In one instance, the "No Popery" forces employed artillery against the defenders of a Catholic church. In the course of the rioting, thirteen persons were killed, scores suffered injuries, the

[13] *Ibid,* p. 525: "Though the Baptists had been the first to advocate religious instruction of the young as against the secularism of the Public School Society, yet as soon as Catholics advocated it, and asked a return to the old New York system, the Protestant denominations, generally, arrayed themselves against the religious education of the young."

Catholic seminary, two churches and whole blocks of Catholic dwellings went up in flame.[14]

The climactic Philadelphia riots were followed by an interval of truce. Responsible Protestants were alienated by this outburst of violence and the attention of the country was drawn to more pressing problems than the perilous plots of Popery. The question of the ownership of Oregon was debated with Great Britain, the problem of the acquisition of Texas was disputed with Mexico, ultimately on the battlefield, and the perennial argument over Negro slavery opened ever wider the chasm between North and South. Within Protestantism, the question of Negro slavery reached the stage of crisis. New York Methodists, dissatisfied with the position of their denomination in the dispute, went into schism and, in 1843, established the Wesleyan Methodist Connection. In 1845 the Methodists of the South prefigured the secession of the Southern States by breaking the communion of the Methodist Episcopal Church and constituting the Methodist Episcopal Church, South. In the same year, Southern Baptists shattered the Baptist confederation and erected their own southern convention.

As the decade of the Forties drew to a close, the stage was once more cleared for the entrance of the Protestant crusaders. The debate over Oregon had been settled by compromise, the war with Mexico had been brought to a most satisfactory termination, and the possibilities of compromise on the slavery question were to be realized in 1850. Once more the spectral shadows of Papal plots and Popish

[14] Cf. Channing, *op. cit.,* V, p. 218 f.; Shea, *op. cit.,* IV, p. 47 ff.

deviltries were cast over the pages of Protestant papers, and the sermons of Protestant ministers.

The renewed campaign against Catholicism was widened to include an attack on the Faith of the Catholic immigrants. The poorer districts of the cities were invaded by the proselytizers of several interdenominational organizations, as well as by the home missionaries of the individual sects. Typical of the interdenominational groups was the American Home and Foreign Christian Union. This society formed in 1849 by an amalgamation of three earlier bodies, the American Protestant Society, the Foreign Evangelical Society and the Christian Alliance, blatantly announced its purpose as "the diffusion of evangelical truth, wherever a corrupted form of Christianity exists, at home and abroad." [15] Needless to say, this corrupt Christianity was Catholicism. Within a remarkably short time, proselytizing stations had been opened in the Catholic sections of cities throughout the United States and the work of converting Catholics to Christianity was prosecuted with large financial support and at times by questionable methods.[16] In spite of the material benefits held out by the proselytizers, their attempts on the Faith of the Catholic immigrants was an egregious failure. Latourette summarizes the results of these Protestant efforts: "It seems clear that in spite of the expenditure by Protestant churches of millions of dollars in religious and social efforts for the immigrants,

[15] Billington, *op. cit.*, p. 442 quotes these words in the constitution of the Union. The author reprints the constitutions of several anti-Catholic societies in his Appendix.

[16] Abel, Theodore, *Protestant Home Missions to Catholic Immigrants*, p. 31 ff.

largely of the Roman Catholic form of the Faith, no large movements of Roman Catholics to Protestantism occurred, the size of most Protestant congregations gathered from Roman Catholic immigrants was small, the growth of such congregations was unimpressive, and many of the converts who were made were unstable in their faith." [17]

While the attack on the immigrants' Faith was beginning, new Papal aggressions stirred the bigots to higher anger. The restoration of the English Catholic Hierarchy, which had been suppressed since the days of Queen Elizabeth, and the "Romanizing" tendencies of the Oxford Movement aroused the apprehensions of further Popish aggressions in this country. The fears of the bigots were realized with the arrival of Bishop Bedini as Apostolic Visitor to the United States in 1852.[18]

With Bedini's arrival, rioting was renewed. Several attempts were made on the Apostolic Visitor's person.[19] Shortly after his departure from a Cincinnati church, the edifice was attacked and burned by a Nativist mob. On another occasion shots were fired into his room and in several instances furious bigots attempted to mob him. Attacks on Catholic institutions again occurred; a number

[17] Latourette, *op. cit.,* IV, p. 283.

Abel, *op. cit.,* p. 33 summarizes the results up to 1933: "If we take the available figures at their face value, the most that can be claimed by American churches engaged in mission work among Catholic immigrants is a total membership of between 50,000 and 60,000. This estimated total includes, besides converts from Catholicism, the children and grandchildren of converts who have not themselves been brought up in Catholicism, and also persons of Protestant stock." The author is by no means inclined to take the figures at their face value.

[18] Cf. Binkley, Wilfred E., *American Political Parties,* p. 189.

[19] Billington, *op. cit.,* p. 392; Shea, *op. cit.,* IV, p. 359 ff.

of churches were burned, others were blown up by gun-
powder, while priests and religious were threatened, as-
saulted, stoned.[20] A Jesuit priest in Maine barely escaped
death as the consequence of a violent physical attack which
culminated in tarring and feathering.[21]

The climax of the new series was reached in the mid
Fifties. A year after rioters in St. Louis killed ten men, the
greatest bloodshed occurred on Louisville's "Bloody Mon-
day" of 1855. After the disorder had died down, the
Catholic Bishop of Louisville sadly reported: "Nearly
a hundred poor Irish and Germans have been butchered
or burned, and some twenty houses have been fired and
burned to the ground. The city authorities, all Know-
Nothings, looked calmly on, and they are now endeavoring
to lay the blame on the Catholics." [22]

While these attacks on Catholic lives and property were
being launched and while the attempt on the Faith of the
Catholic immigrants was in progress, the anti-Catholic
forces mounted potentially the most dangerous attack on
Catholicism in the field of politics. Several Nativist parties
had been organized in the earlier days of the Protestant
Crusade; none, however, proved to be of much consequence. But the political attack reached very formidable
proportions in the heyday of the Know Nothing Party.
The members of this secret society, grandiloquently en-
titled "The Supreme Order of the Star Spangled Banner,"
were inspired by one supreme motivating force. "Only one

[20] Cf. Shea, *loc. cit.*

[21] Less fortunate was a Spanish Franciscan who was killed by American
Nativists in Texas in 1834. Shea, *op. cit.,* IV, p. 714 ff.

[22] Quoted in Shea, *op. cit.,* IV, p. 562.

force held the Know Nothing party together, and that was hatred for the Catholic Church." [23]

This meteoric political party flashed on the national political scene in the elections of 1854, when it demonstrated amazing power at the polls. Since votes were then given *viva voce,* undecided voters may perhaps have been swayed by the presence and the purpose at the polling places of Know Nothing gangs of toughs euphoniously self-styled "Red Necks," "Blood Tubs," "Rough Skins" and "Plug Uglies"; these latter ostentatiously armed with shoemaker's awls.[24] When the votes were tallied, the Know Nothings had elected seventy-five Congressmen and, besides gaining the balance of power in several state legislatures, had won absolute legislative control of nine states. With a justifiable confidence, the party leaders looked forward to the election of their candidate to the White House in the presidential campaign of 1856.

But in its two years of power the party proved only the incapacity of its leadership and the inanity of its politics. Beyond some absurdities, such as the Massachusetts Committee for the Inspection of Nunneries, the Know Nothing legislators achieved nothing.[25]

Before the presidential campaign of 1856 was begun, the dazzling power of the Know Nothing party had been dissipated. Its legislative failure, the dissensions in its ranks,

[23] Billington, *op. cit.,* p. 387.

[24] Binkley, *op. cit.,* p. 189.

[25] For a description of this Committee in action, cf. Whipple, Leon, *Story of Civil Liberty in the U.S.,* p. 59 ff. In other fields, however, the Know Nothings attained a measure of success. MacLeod, "Contacts," p. 1041, attributes the massacres of defenseless Oregon Indians to these Nativists.

the criticism and ridicule to which it offered a splendid target, the popular reaction to the arson and bloodshed which it encouraged, all contributed to the quick collapse of the organization. Finally, the supreme cause of the eclipse of Nativism was operative. Only in times of peace can the United States afford the luxury of anti-Catholicism; before the very real and awful spectre of civil war, the Catholic bogeyman vanished.

CHAPTER VII

THE PROBLEM OF THE NEGRO

WHILE the floodtide of religious bigotry was penetrating the remotest backwaters of the United States, the problem of Negro slavery was gathering a tidal wave of forces destined to overwhelm the peace-seeking elements of the nation, to plunge the country into a terrible war and ultimately to destroy the social and economic foundations of the South. As we know to our sorrow, even the sacrifices and bloodshed of a fratricidal war solved but the first of many problems of racial relationships.

In the bright dawn of our history as an independent nation when all things seemed possible, it appeared that Negro slavery was doomed to an early extinction. By the close of the 18th Century the economic disadvantages of the institution in the Northern States had there destined slavery to an early natural end. In those early days a number of the smaller Protestant denominations had gone on record in opposition to the slave trade and even to slavery itself.

But in the first decades of the 19th Century Protestant opposition to the enslavement of human beings was apparently stilled. Only a few ineffectual voices were raised among the Northern congregations in condemnation of the inhuman system. The denominations of the South, after the invention of the cotton gin and the rise of the Cotton Kingdom, silently or vocally approved the South's peculiar institution. Sweet writes: "Apart from its moral and religious aspects, nowhere can there be found a better example of the influence exerted upon organized Christianity by economic conditions than is furnished by a study of the relations of the churches to slavery. It was not until church members had become wealthy cotton growers that the churches ceased to denounce the institution." [1] Even the sects so lately formed among the lower economic classes of the South and mid-West did not oppose the continued enslavement of the Negroes. Channing writes of the Methodists, Baptists and Presbyterians: "In the first decades (of the 19th Century), these churches were either silent as to slavery, or pro-slavery. The Methodists omitted from their discipline Wesley's prohibition of the ownership of man and for a long time the opposition to slave holding on the part of clergy and laity was confined to New England and New York." [2]

As the century advanced, however, anti-slavery sentiment, nourished largely on Christian principles, grew ever stronger in the North. Sincere Christian men and women risked their lives to construct and operate the "Underground Railroad" and to propagandize the cause of abolition. More and more leaders of Northern Protestantism identified themselves with the proponents of Negro freedom, and in the pulpits of Northern churches increasing

[1] Sweet, *Story,* p. 6.
[2] Channing, *op. cit.,* V, p. 227.

numbers of anti-slavery sermons were pronounced. Unfortunately the bitter spirit of the rabid abolitionists increasingly permeated the Northern Protestant pronouncements. The growing virulence of Northern Protestant attacks on the peculiar institution was answered by equally violent and abusive rebuttals from Southern church leaders. Southern Protestantism became increasingly identified with the slave system. "By the opening of the Civil War, the churches had become the chief bulwarks of slavery." [3]

The Catholic Church remained largely untouched by this conflict within organized Christianity. Some members, both clerical and lay, of the Catholic groups in Maryland and southern Louisiana were slave-owners; and some clergymen spoke in defense of slavery.[4] But since the overwhelming majority of Catholic church membership was concentrated in the North, the question of slavery was not a major problem among Catholics. The Church, engaged in a struggle for its very existence with the anti-Catholic forces of the United States, had little time or energy to devote to the question. The unrestrained violence of the Abolitionists had little appeal for Catholics who were experiencing examples of Nativist violence; and the knowledge that large Abolitionist support came from the ranks of the anti-Catholic bigots was, in itself, enough to warn Catholics to caution.

The Catholic Church, therefore, confronted by the attacks

[3] Sweet, *loc. cit.* Cf. Garrison, Winfred E., *The March of Faith*, p. 16 ff.; Buck, Paul H., *The Road to Reunion*, p. 58.

[4] For examples of Catholic opinion and practise in the slavery question, cf. Rice, Madeleine H., *American Catholic Opinion in the Slavery Controversy, passim;* Embree, Edwin R., *Brown Americans*, p. 51 ff.

of the Nativists and the tremendous problems of administration and service posed by the immigrants, did not undertake a solution of the Negro problem as such. It strove, however, to mitigate the abuses inherent in the institution of slavery. A recent author has summed up the Catholic position: "Toward the existent system of Negro slavery the Church officially maintained its traditional attitude of 1) alleviating the hardships connected with it, 2) protecting the integrity of family life and safeguarding the natural rights of the slave, 3) insisting upon religious equality and sufficient instruction to insure an understanding of the fundamental truths of religion, 4) encouraging manumission. [5]

Before mid-century, the problem of slavery had produced a state of crisis in Protestantism. As abusive charge was answered by violent countercharge, the Protestant denominations began to break asunder on sectional lines. The Methodist and Baptist communions were ruptured in the mid-Forties. When the clouds of approaching civil war darkened the horizon, other denominations followed the example of the Evangelicals. It is a rather sad commentary that "Faiths which had once been bonds of national communion had now become agencies of discord." [6] The example of the denominations in severing that first and most important connection between North and South, the religious union in the churches of Christ, could not but influence the political leaders of the South.[7]

[5] Rice, *op. cit.*, p. 21.   [6] Buck, *op. cit.*, p. 58.

[7] It is not clear how much influence the congregational polity of the Baptists, largest of the Southern denominations, had on the States' Rights theory of the Southerners.

When finally the irrepressible conflict was debated on the battlefield, "the various denominations, as was to be expected, showed themselves to be the mouthpieces of the economic and sectional groups they represented." [8] With the outbreak of the war, the last major Protestant denominations broke into sectional sects; but one major Christian denomination escaped the destruction of its communion. "Throughout the great struggle, the Catholics arose above the schism of the nation." [9]

As the war progressed, the Protestant churches assumed a leading role in its support. "It is no exaggeration to affirm that the churches in both sections became the chief recruiting agencies and the chief builders of morals." [10] Inevitably the influence of the Catholic Church was solicited by both warring governments. Archbishop Hughes, who at the height of the Protestant crusade had refused a Federal request to negotiate with the Mexican government, was dispatched by Lincoln on a mission to insure the continued neutrality of France and England. Similarly Jefferson Davis sent Bishop Lynch of Charleston, to offset Federal recruiting in Ireland and to represent the Confederate cause at the Holy See. While Catholics in both North and South rallied to the support of their respective governments, the Church, generally speaking, played no important part in the continuation of the war.

When the last remnants of Lee's shattered armies surrendered and the work of reconstruction was begun, Protes-

---

[8] Niebuhr, *op. cit.,* p. 24; Cf. Woodson, *op. cit.,* p. 591.

[9] Weigle, *op. cit.,* p. 7.

[10] Buck, *op. cit.,* p. 60.

tantism continued the schism caused by slavery and war. Throughout the era of Reconstruction, "the churches remained sectional bodies, an antagonistic element in the integration of national life. Not only did the work of religion and social improvement suffer from the lack of harmony, the future was also to reveal the sorry spectacle of clergymen standing as the most radical of the sectionalists." [11]

Among the numerous factors which contributed to the continued division of Protestantism, the bitterness caused by the war and its aftermath may be considered the chief. The seizure of Southern church edifices by Northern clergymen in the wake of victorious Federal armies could scarcely further denominational reunion.[12] When in the period of Reconstruction ill-advised Northern ministers advocated racial intermarriage and lauded the Carpetbaggers as "the true knight-errantry of the age," wounded Southern sensibilities were not thereby solaced. When Northern sects adopted the policy of regarding the former Confederate States as a mission field, and dispatched missionaries to convert not only the Negro freedmen but the whites, the white Southerners were very understandably indignant; many Negroes, however, were profoundly touched by the daring of missionaries who risked their lives to instruct them.[13]

The identification of the Northern denominations with the Republican party and with the Reconstruction policies

[11] *Ibid*, p. 66.
[12] *Ibid*, p. 61.
[13] *Ibid*, p. 62.

of the Republican radicals led to a similar identification of the Southern sects with the Democratic party.[14] The industrial development of the North in the latter decades of the 19th Century produced economic interests which clashed with the interests of the agricultural South; and the sects, always sensitive to the economic concerns of their membership, reflected the viewpoints of the sectional groups they represented. The theological basis of reunion was gradually destroyed as the more bourgeois Northern sects increasingly advocated the liberal Protestant theology, and the less prosperous Southern denominations became the stronghold of the older Protestant orthodoxy.[15]

As a consequence of these factors, the sectional division in Protestantism between North and South has perdured. In the era of Reconstruction only one schismatic group, the Protestant Episcopal Church of the Confederate States of America, rejoined its parent body. The first reunion of the Northern and Southern components of an Evangelical denomination did not take place until, in 1939, the Southern Methodists rejoined their Northern coreligionists. Most schisms caused by the slavery question and the Civil War still exist.

The era of Reconstruction not only failed to witness a reconstructed Protestant unity, but the same age saw the opening of a new and enduring fissure in Protestantism, the separation of the Negro Christians from the churches of the whites.

It is impossible to determine how many Negroes were

[14] Sweet, *Story*, p. 470.
[15] Hall, *op. cit.*, p. 292.

Christians before the Civil War. The Negroes, as slaves everywhere, tended to adopt the *mores* and the religion of the dominant class. Some slave owners provided for the religious instruction of their servants and arranged for the attendance of their colored people at white Christian services. It can be disputed whether the masters pursued this latter course because of the Pauline condemnation of distinctions between bond and free, or because of fears that all-Negro churches would foster discontent and rebellion.[16] Certain it is that exclusively colored congregations were discouraged. After Nat Turner's slave rebellion. "the rumor attached to Negro ministers throughout the South the stigma of using preaching as a means to incite their race to insurrection." [17] Prohibitions against Negro churches were enacted into state law; one legislature forbade more than five Negroes to attend religious services, "except when conducted by a recognized white minister or attended by at least two discreet and reputable persons." [18] Negro Christians, therefore, could not freely evangelize their racial brethren, and white church leaders did not fully realize the potentialities of the colored mission field. As a consequence, "at the time of Emancipation probably only a minority of the Negro slaves were nominal Christians." [19]

All-Negro denominations, nevertheless, had come into existence before the Civil War; but their congregations were confined to the Northern States and their member-

[16] Niebuhr, *op. cit.,* p. 250 ff.; Myrdal, Gunnar, *An American Dilemma,* II, p. 859.
[17] Mays, Benjamin E. and Nicholson, J. W., *The Negro's Church,* p. 29.
[18] Embree, *op. cit.,* p. 54.
[19] Myrdal, *op. cit.,* II, p. 860.

ship was composed of manumitted Negroes and their children. Two of the largest colored sects, the African Methodist Episcopal Church and the African Methodist Episcopal Zion Church, had been established about 1820 as a consequence of the objections of Northern whites to the presence of Negroes at divine services.

The most impressive religious developments in the South during the period of Reconstruction were the abandonment of the Southern denominations by the great majority of their Negro communicants and the enormous growth of the colored sects.[20] The Methodist Episcopal Church, South, for example, lost more than three-quarters of its 200,000 Negro church members in the year following Appomatox. The African Methodist-Episcopal Church, which had not existed in the slave States, found the majority of its 400,000 church members in 1880 below the Mason-Dixon Line. In one decade of Reconstruction the African Methodist Episcopal Zion Church enrolled 150,000 new members in territory formerly forbidden to its preachers. The major gains, however, were reaped by the Negro Baptists. Due largely to the emotional and dramatic appeal of their services, particularly of their baptismal rite, Baptist ministers gained an absolute majority of the new members of the colored sects. To the present day, Negro Baptists number half of all colored American Christians and form by far the largest colored denomination in the United States.[21]

Several factors contributed to this great migration from

[20] The Catholic Church also suffered some loss of membership. Cf. Gillard, *The Catholic Church and the American Negro,* p. 258; also his *Colored Catholics in the United States,* p. 100 ff.

[21] Cf. Bass, *op. cit.,* p. 319, for a survey of Negro church statistics.

the white to the colored sects. In the first flush of emancipation, the Negroes understandably sought and seized every opportunity to control their own institutional life, to exercise hitherto denied abilities for leadership, and to manifest their complete independence of the whites. The Negro sects offered a shining chance to satisfy these natural desires. Further, Christianity under white leadership had notably failed to erase the color line. The colored man was cognizant of the fact that he was rather tolerated in than sought by the white Christian denominations. For the white congregations generally excluded colored members from their social and recreational activities, segregated them from the whites at divine services, and offered them little opportunity for the exercise of the ministry. Again, the white Protestant sects had little appeal for the Negro. The non-Evangelical denominations were not equipped to satisfy the peculiar religious needs of the colored people, who were, it must be remembered, members of the lower economic classes, almost universally poverty-stricken and uneducated. While the white Evangelical sects of the South lagged behind the bourgeois developments of their Northern co-religionists, they had, nevertheless, reached such a point in their evolution into sects of the middle-class that they could no longer supply the emotional appeal that characterized their conquest of the frontier.

So the Negro sects prospered. Their growth followed rather closely the typical pattern of Evangelicalism which had been manifested in the Great Awakening and the evangelization of the frontier. Revivals once more were common occurrences, and scenes of mass hysteria were repeated.[22] The growing colored denominations manifested all the characteristics of sects of the lower economic classes: the emphasis on "conversion," emotional worship, millennarianism, the Puritan code of behavior.

In one respect, however, the Negro denominations have not followed the typical Evangelical pattern. Since after three generations of freedom the colored people, due to circumstances largely out of their control, have not developed a sufficiently large middle-class, the Negro Evangelical denominations of today are still sects of the lower economic classes, with the doctrine and the worship of primitive Evangelical sects.[23]

Only a few denominations under control of the whites succeeded in salvaging any appreciable numbers of their ante-bellum Negro constituency. Today but three Protestant sects have more than a handful of colored members. It may be significant that these three—the Protestant Episcopal Church, the Presbyterian Church, U.S.A., and the Disciples of Christ—are rather Northern than Southern sects, and that none of these interracial churches apparently encourages biracial services.[24] The continued importance of the

[22] Bowers, Claude G., *The Tragic Era,* p. 49 f.

[23] Mays and Nicholson, *op. cit.,* p. 282; Embree, *op. cit.,* p. 190 f.; Myrdal, *op. cit.,* II, p. 936 ff.; Frazier, E. Franklin, *Negro Youth at the Crossways,* p. 112 *et passim.*

[24] Johnson, Charles S., *Patterns of Negro Segregation,* p. 276: "There are not many church denominations in the South in which Negro and white worship in the same building. The Catholic Churches permit or encourage biracial worship more often than the Protestant. The Primitive Baptists continue the practise of joint worship in some small Southern communities." The author gives no further examples of interracial worship.

color line in Protestantism is indicated by the fact that, in the recent great movement towards the reunion of Protestantism, no noteworthy attempts have been made to reunite the white and colored churches.

But while Protestantism has failed to obliterate the color line, it has performed a notable apostolate in the education of the Negro. The truly remarkable educational progress accomplished by the Negro American has been due largely to the admirable achievements and the devoted personnel of Protestant educational institutions.

The aftermath of the Civil War had far less repercussions within Catholicism. Of approximately 100,000 Negro Catholics, possibly a fifth drifted away from the Church; and Gillard attributes their defection to neglect rather than to apostasy.[25] The promising mission field offered by the newly freed Negroes was largely left uncultivated by the Church, engrossed in other business. In recent decades, however, the labors of those unique congregations of Negro nuns, the Oblate Sisters of Providence and the Sisters of the Holy Family, have been seconded by numbers of white sisterhoods and smaller groups of colored Religious. Increasing numbers of priests, diocesan and Religious, notably Josephite, Divine Word and Holy Ghost Fathers, have devoted themselves to work for the Negroes. Their labors are bearing fruit; Negro Catholics in the United States now number over 300,000.[26] The Catholic Church has long been the Church of the majority of Negro Christians in the

[25] Gillard, *Colored Catholics*, p. 103.
[26] LaFarge, John, *The Race Question and the Negro*, p. 44. Cf. Myrdal, *op. cit.*, II, p. 864 n.

world.[27] Since today possibly half the Negro membership of all predominantly white American churches is Catholic, it may be asserted that the Catholic Church is the major interracial Church in the United States.

Even while the churches and the nation were struggling with the problems posed by slavery, the Civil War and Reconstruction, the ebullition of movements on the lunatic fringe of religion continued. The most remarkable development of the times was the tremendous but ephemeral growth, due partly to the strain of the war years, of the fad of Spiritualism. Between 1850 and 1872 more than 2,000 Spiritualist congregations were formed.[28] Even before the outbreak of the war, partisans of the movement claimed the conversion to Spiritualism of 2,000,000 people.[29] While the fad became increasingly fashionable during the war, the usual frauds perpetrated by the swarms of "mediums," who sprang into being to cater to the craze, soon cast disrepute on the whole of the Spiritualistic movement. By the decade of the Eighties, the "spirits" could summon but a few remnants of their once large following.

While the multitude of Protestant sects was being increased by the emergence of many new Negro denominations, still more sects reached this country from Europe. The esoteric Catholic Apostolic Church, whose members are better known as Irvingites, sent over some believers and an "Apostle" or two; within a few years the American

---

[27] LaFarge, *op. cit.,* p. 22, cites an estimate of 20,000,000 Negro Catholics in the world.

[28] Lyon, *op. cit.,* p. 231.

[29] Sweet, *Story,* p. 404; Weigle, *op. cit.,* p. 172.

branch of this English sect had produced the inevitable schism. From England also came the Plymouth Brethren, or Darbyites, who were founded to unite all Christians in one church and showed the way by splitting into eight minuscule sects. The Mennonites, who in this period sloughed off four sects in this country, welcomed from Europe four more divisions of their small group: the *Kleine Gemeinde,* the Hutterian Brethren, the *Bruder Gemeinde* and the *Krimmer Bruder Gemeinde.*

CHAPTER VIII

THE INCREASE OF UNBELIEF

WHILE churchmen, at the release of each new estimate of church membership and the publication of each new series of church statistics, are prone to point with pride to increases in church membership, it is extremely doubtful whether, in the long view, Christianity is maintaining its hold on the people of the United States.[1] Certainly no one can speak of the 20th Century as Rowe wrote of the last: "Americans of the 19th Century were on the whole a church-going people, at least in the older sections of the country." [2] American Christianity would appear to have lost rather than gained ground in the past century, if Channing's estimate is true: "Probably it would not be far out of the way to set down three-quarters of the inhabitants of the United States as belonging to some Christian organization in 1850, or at all events as considering themselves within the Christian fold." [3] There can be no doubt that, while the membership of the churches may have kept pace with population growth, the numbers of infidels have multiplied again and again in the past three generations.

The closing decades of the 19th Century form a period

[1] Cf. Swift, Arthur L., *New Frontiers of Religion*, p. 74.
[2] Rowe, *op. cit.*, p. 123.
[3] Channing, *op. cit.*, V, p. 220.

in which the growth of infidelity is marked. Two other important movements within Protestantism are notable: the marked growth of the liberal Protestant theology, and the closer identification of the sects with the economic and social classes of their constituency.[4]

While the factors which initiated the liberalizing trend in theology continued operative throughout the century, in the latter decades probably the most important solvent of the ancient orthodoxy was provided by the "Science versus Religion" controversy, precipitated by the popularization of Darwin's theory of evolution, the new study of comparative religion and the "Higher Criticism" of the Holy Scriptures. The immediate and at times uncritical acceptance of the pronunciamentos of "science" by many churchmen, both clerics and laymen, led inevitably to the abandonment of dogmas ostensibly in conflict with the findings of science and to disdain for orthodox theology in general.

The advance of the new theology was gradual, permeating some sects, particularly those of the upper-classes, more quickly than others. While it is difficult to determine the precise moment when a sect had completely relinquished the older orthodoxy, the denominations of Calvinistic provenance seem to have led the way.[5] In his *Study of the*

---

[4] For a similar growth of liberal theology in European Protestantism, cf. Hayes, Carleton J. H., *A Generation of Materialism,* p. 124 ff.

[5] Latourette, *op. cit.,* IV, p. 431: "Yet long before the close of the 19th Century, except for conservative minorities, they (the Calvinistic sects) had largely abandoned some of the most striking features of that system." Garrison, *op. cit.,* p. 188, writes of the originally Calvinistic Unitarians: "Since 1894, or even a little earlier, the chief emphasis has been upon ethical culture and upon those universal elements which Christianity holds in common with other great religions."

Christian Sects published in 1896, Lyon writes: "The study of this subject and the conversations I have had with various representative men have surprised me by revealing the state of confusion and change in which all beliefs, except those of the Roman Catholics, now exist. Few of those who claim to hold the faith of their fathers are aware how far they have drifted from that faith." [6]

As early as 1880 many ministers and church members were in substantial agreement with the statement of a clergyman representing the liberal school:

"The sections of that theology which treat of sin and salvation they (the Liberals) regard as especially untenable. These sections comprehend the following doctrines: the descent of man from Adam . . . the fall of Adam . . . the imputation of Adam's guilt to his posterity . . . the redemption in Christ . . . the quickening in the elect of a new life—at their baptism, Catholics affirm—at the moment of their conversion, most Protestants allege; the eternal punishment of those who remain unregenerate. . . .

"These sections of the traditional theology of Christendom . . . dominated the Christian intellect for centuries. They have ceased to dominate it. They no longer press on the minds and spirits of men like an incubus." [7]

While these heterodox opinions were finding ever wider acceptance within the Protestant denominations, other and more radical ideas gained Protestant partisans. As the years advanced, more and more members of the sects questioned

[6] Lyon, *op. cit.*, quoted in 13th edition, iii. The editor adds the words: "This confusion still exists."

[7] Quoted in Bonham, John M., *Secularism, Its Progress and Its Morals*, p. 118.

and denied the inerrancy and the divine authorship of the Bible, the doctrines of the Trinity and the Incarnation. Some liberals moved from a denial of the Three Persons in God to a denial of a personal God; they directed their prayers—if they prayed—to "the Great Reality" or "the Soul of the Universe." Many who admitted a personal God denied that He was infinite; Christians refused to concede to Christ a miraculous power to cure and denied to an almighty Law-giver the ability to suspend His laws. Many of the more advanced liberals advocated the pantheistic doctrine of the "immanence of God." Others attributed to God but a conceptual existence; they considered Him a mere symbol, which existed only when men thought about Him.[8] These are but some of the vagaries which found adherents among the clergy and laity of the Protestant denominations.[9]

While the liberal theology was destroying the historic beliefs of the Protestant churches, the immutable doctrines of the Catholic Church, strongly reaffirmed by the Vatican Council of 1870, were maintained in their fulness by American Catholics. Other non-Protestants, however, did not escape the deleterious effects of the novel ideas on their

---

[8] Latourette, *op. cit.*, IV, p. 434: "As the decades passed, a minority in several denominations of Calvinist provenance became extreme humanists. They not only abandoned the doctrine of election, but also rejected the sovereignty and even the independent existence of God. To them, God became a symbol of the highest human aspirations and without reality apart from the minds of men. Interestingly enough, a chief center of this view was in the University of Chicago, an institution founded by the formerly Calvinistic Baptists."

[9] For a fuller treatment of the liberal theology, cf. Rowe, *op. cit.*, p. 132 ff.

historic beliefs. The Jews, whose numbers were substantially increased in the course of the New Immigration, proved susceptible to the new concepts. Some of the more advanced abandoned the Mosaic religion and founded the American Ethical Union. Others surrendered hope in the coming of the Messiah and, retaining only the moral precepts, gave up the ritualistic ordinations of the Mosaic Law. These Reform Jews banded together in the Union of American Hebrew Congregations, while the Orthodox Jews established the Union of Orthodox Jewish Congregations and the moderates erected the United Synagogue of America.

Orthodox Protestants viewed with disquietude the advance of liberalism, and united their efforts in combating the trend. Particularly in the early days of the liberalizing trend was the reaction of the adherents of the older faith strong. While orthodox control of the denominations was maintained, the liberals were given short shrift; "heresy trials" were prosecuted, and the unwelcome radicals were defrocked and "disfellowshipped." [10]

When, regardless of their efforts, the advance of liberalism continued, the orthodox were forced to employ other methods. As seminary after seminary went over to the liberal side, new schools of orthodoxy were established to

[10] For examples, cf. Schlesinger, Arthur M., "Critical Period in American Religion: 1875-1900," p. 7 ff.; Beardsley, Frank G., *History of Christianity in America,* p. 212 ff. Fry, C. Luther, "Changes in Religious Organizations," *Recent Social Trends,* II, p. 1011: "A detailed analysis of the heresy cases during the past forty years reveals that the number of cases has been dwindling and that in recent years only a few of those that have actually been tried have resulted in convictions, thus indicating a changing attitude on the part of church authorities towards the beliefs of the clergy."

train ministers in the "old time" religion.[11] The orthodox sought recruits for their forces through the labors of professional evangelists; they met in interdenominational Bible congresses and conferences; they made the pulpits in their power platforms for polemical preaching.[12]

The fact is significant that the new theology did not, save in a few instances of very minor importance, cause the disruption of the sects. In the same church edifices, whether they were Episcopalian, Presbyterian or Baptist, the orthodox and the liberal participated in the same services. The liberal did not advert to the anomaly of worshiping beside an idolator who gave divine adoration to the mere man, Christ. Nor did the orthodox perceive his false position in offering joint prayers with a kind of atheist, who denied the Godhead incarnate in Christ.[13]

Together with the advance of the liberal Protestant theology went the ever closer identification of the denominations with special groups. "The urban era opened with the Protestant churches slipping into a passive alliance with

[11] Cole, Stewart G., *History of Fundamentalism,* p. 421: "Practically all the well-known seminaries in the north experienced a liberalizing conversion, in spite of the efforts of orthodox leaders. . . ."

[12] Cole, *op. cit.,* Chapter III, gives a full account of the orthodox campaign.

[13] It appears that this anomalous position perdures. Fry, "Changes," p. 1011: "In many local churches, Protestant ministers are faced with the dilemma of preaching to congregations that are partly fundamentalist and partly liberal. Often members of the same congregation differ more widely than do the creeds of separate denominations on such questions as the Virgin Birth, the deity of Christ and his resurrection from the dead. Walter Lippmann in his *A Preface to Morals* quotes the president of the Fundamentalist Association as saying that nothing holds the liberals and fundamentalists together save the billions of dollars invested in church property."

the well-to-do middle classes." [14] The rising capitalist assumed a dominant position in the councils of the sects. The big business men became the leading figures in their congregations. Their contributions erected splendid church edifices, paid professional choirs, reimbursed the labors of the ministers. Rich industrialists and financiers assumed control of church finances, educational institutions, mission boards. They even found time to inspire the young with tales of their achievements; Rockefeller was not the only millionaire to tell a Sunday School class how God gave him his money. To those outside the pale of organized Christianity, many Protestant congregations appeared the preserves of the wealthy.

The pulpit reflected the changing financial background of the sect members. "The 'consecration of wealth' became a favorite topic of edifying discourse." [15] Pulpit orators taught a strange new "gospel of wealth" which imposed an obligation on Christians to get rich and to hold their wealth as stewards of the Lord. This "gospel of wealth" was, "in effect, a Protestant strategem to retain for itself a place in the new social order, to provide itself with a function, in short, to save itself as a significant social institution. Urban Protestantism cultivated the middle and upper-classes who possessed the ultimate power in American society." [16] Nor was the preaching of the "gospel of wealth" restricted to the pulpits of the non-Evangelical sects. "Even the Baptist and Methodist faiths, once religions of the poor,

[14] Abell, Aaron I., *The Urban Impact on American Protestantism*, p. 246.

[15] Garrison, *op. cit.*, p. 229.

[16] Gabriel, *op. cit.*, p. 157.

now displayed almost frantic solicitude for the spiritual welfare of the rich." [17]

While the sects were cultivating the rich, the poor suffered from neglect. A Protestant writer asserts: "In fact, the Protestant churches for over a century have been in a constant condition of flight from the common people. Where poor people, or foreigners, or Jews moved in, the Protestant churches moved out." [18] In a forty-year period after the Civil War, lower New York City witnessed a tremendous increase in population and the exodus of no fewer than seventy-two Protestant churches and missions.[19] Not only did the sects abandon the urban masses, but in the labor conflicts of the period they appeared as the champions of the rich. "The pulpit, increasingly beholden to contributions of the rich, ordinarily ignored or condoned the terrible injustices from which the wage-earning multitudes were suffering . . ." [20]

The consequences of the union of Protestantism and wealth are apparent: "as the cities became numerous and powerful, the churches lost the major part of their wage-earning members and failed to recoup their losses from the enlarging immigrant population." [21] Migrants from the Protestant rural districts of America and immigrants from the Protestant lands of Europe witnessed the exodus of the Protestant sects from the lower-class sections of the cities. The union members among them heard Samuel Gompers'

---

[17] Abell, *op. cit.*, p. 4.
[18] Baker, Roy S., *The Spiritual Unrest*, p. 69.
[19] *Ibid*, p. 71.
[20] Schlesinger, *op. cit.*, p. 11.
[21] Abell, *op. cit.*, p. 246.

blunt charge that the intellect and talent of the ministry had been suborned by the plutocratic oppressors of the poor,[22] and they were urged by their leaders to abandon Protestant Christianity.[23] They heard preached in the few churches that remained with them a doctrine geared only to the mentality of the bourgeoisie.[24] It is very understandable, therefore, that "the outstanding and appalling fact was simply that the masses of the people, particularly the laboring classes, were callously indifferent to the ministrations of the Protestant churches." [25] By the thousands and scores of thousands, the lower economic classes abandoned a Protestantism which had first abandoned them.

In brilliant contrast to the Protestant dereliction was the record of Catholicism. While the Protestant churches were following the middle-class Americans to the suburbs and the better residential wards of the cities, the Catholic Church, with small means and at great expense—for slum property is notoriously expensive—erected churches and schools to care for the inhabitants of the lower-class districts. The emergence of the Catholic Church in 1890 with the most numerous church membership in the United States, a great proportion of which was composed of the

[22] Schlesinger, *op. cit.,* p. 5; cf. Abell, *op. cit.,* p. 63 f.

[23] Abell, *op. cit.,* p. 10. Cf. Gabriel, *op. cit.,* p. 181.

[24] Garrison, *op. cit.,* p. 123: "The changes . . . matched the mood of the prosperous bourgeoisie, but a large constituency was left behind, including, first, those who were capable neither of following a thoughtful sermon nor of appreciating a dignified and restrained service; and, second, the less fortunate element among the industrial workers and those who were more concerned about the economic betterment of labor than about the promotion of the church. . . ."

[25] Hopkins, Charles H., *The Rise of the Social Gospel,* p. 103.

immigrants and their progeny, bears witness to the success of Catholicism with the problem of the urban proletariat. In the test applied by the slums the superiority of Catholicism over Protestantism is apparent.

The great apostasy of the times was not restricted to the cities and towns of the nation. While urban Protestantism was deserting the masses, the rural masses were deserting Protestantism.

The great migration from the countryside which made 20th Century America a predominantly urban nation emptied the pews of many rural Protestant churches. As congregations dwindled, hundreds and thousands of church edifices were closed.[26] In a desperate attempt to keep organized Christianity alive, many groups abandoned their particular creeds and united in federated or community churches, while other groups merged their diminished numbers with neighboring congregations of the same denomination.[27]

Nor was the recession of Christianity in the rural areas, traditionally the stronghold of Protestantism, due merely to the migration to the cities. The rise in the agricultural districts of a new group of Evangelical denominations, the "Holiness" sects, indicates that even rural Protestantism was

[26] This movement is continuing. Beardsley, *History of Christianity,* p. 236: "One of the disturbing tendencies of the times has been the decline of the rural church. Within recent years many hundreds, if not thousands, of little rural churches, all over the country and representing all denominations, have passed out of existence." For a discussion of the parlous position of present-day rural Protestantism, cf. Douglass, H. Paul and Brenner, Edmund de S., *The Protestant Church as a Social Institution,* p. 66 ff.; Hooker, Elizabeth R., *Hinterlands of the Church, passim.*

[27] Hooker, Elizabeth R., *United Churches,* p. 23 ff.; Bass, *op. cit.,* p. 166 ff.

becoming vitiated by the bourgeois malaise and was losing
its appeal to the lower economic classes. While many immigrants were content to remain in the cities, millions of
European Protestants, notably the Scandinavians, found
their way into the rural areas and out of the Protestant
churches. Writing of the Lutherans, probably the sect most
successful in retaining the allegiance of its European immigrants, Garrison declares: "The church lost heavily by the
failure of its immigrants to keep the faith. In 1897 it was
estimated that one-third of the Norwegians and Swedes in
the United States were still church members, but only one-
twelfth of the Danes." [28]

The latter years of the 19th Century presented a new
phenomenon in the history of American Christianity. For
the first time the lower economic classes, in seeking to
satisfy their emotional needs and express their aspirations,
turned away from the churches. Instead of Christ, the working classes sought out Marx; instead of the emergence of a
new church of the disinherited came the growth of radi-
calism.

True, a typical movement of the Evangelical type of
Protestantism made its appearance about 1875.[29] This
"Holiness" movement produced scores of minuscule sects
distinguished usually by the inclusion of "Pentecostal,"
"Evangelical" or "Holiness" in their titles. But these small

[28] Garrison, *op. cit.,* p. 140.

[29] Garrison, *op. cit.,* p. 181, expresses a rather supercilious view of the
many Holiness sects which arose as schisms from Methodism: "The
cultural advance of Methodism has been facilitated by the sloughing off of
this element among which a fiery religion is compensatory for the
consciousness of financial, social and intellectual inferiority."

denominations generally found their small strength confined to the rural areas and recruited from the membership of the established churches (particularly the Methodist) and not from the "unchurched." [30] Since only a few sects of the Holiness group found their way into the slum districts of the great cities, the movement had little effect on urban infidelity. Most notable of urban Holiness sects was the Salvation Army, the militaristic English importation, noted for its "war" on "Slumdom, Bumdom, and Rumdom." [31] Several of these Holiness sects have already experienced the classical evolutionary process of Evangelical Protestantism. The Church of the Nazarene, for example, has marked its arrival among the sects of the middle-class by quietly dropping the betraying prefix "Pentecostal" from its title.

The extent of the infidelity of the masses was brought home to the churches by the statistics of the religious census taken in 1890 by Federal officials. This first government census, unreliable though it is, nevertheless clearly indicated an enormous number of the "unchurched" in the United States: of a total population of 69,947,714 Americans, 41,248,282 had no connection with organized Christianity. No matter how large a margin for error should be allowed, the census pointed out one inescapable fact: the United States was populated largely by infidels.

The growth of infidelity was accompanied by another rather novel development on the American religious scene,

[30] Clark, *op. cit.,* p. 92 ff.
[31] On the Salvation Army and its schisms, cf. Beardsley, *History of Christianity,* p. 207 ff.

the emergence of a new sect of the upper-classes. To the present day opinions about the new religion and its founder are most varied. "To some of her followers (Mrs. Eddy) has appeared as nothing less than a Christ Incarnate. Other observers have portrayed her as a bigger humbug than Barnum and the worst virago since Xantippe." [32] Estimates of the value of Christian Science have run the gamut from the lauds of its faithful to appraisals such as Ferguson's: "The most that can be said for Christian Science is that it has invested drugless healing with blue lights and incense." [33] It has practically become a cliché among its critics to say that Christian Science is neither Christian nor scientific.

Certainly the life and actions of Mrs. Mary Baker Glover Patterson Eddy present some strange aspects. While she apparently developed her religion from the teachings of an earlier faith-healer, she strenuously denied the debt. [34] While the teachings of Christian Science condemned the employment of physicians, for neither diseases nor human bodies have any real existence, Mrs. Eddy did not hesitate, it is alleged, to consult doctors and to use drugs to relieve her own pains. [35] It appears that Mrs. Eddy considered her own writings inspired equally with the Bible by her pantheistic "Father-Mother God"; certainly she did not hesitate to compose several improved revisions of the Lord's Prayer. [36]

[32] Dakin, Edwin F., *Mrs. Eddy*, p. vii.
[33] Ferguson, *The Confusion of Tongues*, p. 179.
[34] Dakin, *op. cit.*, p. 44 ff.; p. 92 ff.; p. 111 ff.; p. 144 ff.
[35] *Ibid*, pp. 19, 61, 149, 277, *et passim*.
[36] *Ibid.*, p. 245: "She even ventured in the *Journal* of October 1890 to

Over her followers Mrs. Eddy exercised an autocratic rule, marked by sudden and erratic changes of policy.[37] Potential rivals for supremacy were ousted by excommunications, and "heresy" was avoided by regulations forbidding the preaching of original sermons. The office of ministers was supplied in the Christian Science church by "readers," whose task was to present, without interpretations, selected passages of the Bible and Mrs. Eddy's writings.

It appears strange that the new religion gained adherents chiefly among the educated and wealthy classes in the United States.[38] Perhaps the significance of the sect, whose educated members are willing to deny the very existence of the material universe and the reality of the prime facts of human consciousness, is to emphasize, by example, the tendencies of bourgeois Protestantism.[39]

On the other extreme of the social scale appeared sects with beliefs as unusual as those of Christian Science. One Negro Holiness denomination, The Churches of God and Saints of Christ, teaches that the colored race descended from the Ten Lost Tribes of Israel; and another Negro sect affirms that Christ was a Negro. Several small sects show as little regard for natural sciences as Christian Science. The Church Triumphant received by divine revelation a new religion called "Koreshanity"; this strange syncretism taught, besides metempsychosis, astrology and alchemy, the

instruct her students to lay aside the Bible itself in devoting their energies to a study of her own books."

[37] *Ibid,* p. 259 ff., *et passim.*

[38] *Ibid.,* p. 115: ". . . poverty in one of her followers came to be regarded as an error as serious as sickness or sin."

[39] For contrasting studies of Christian Science, cf. Ferguson, *loc. cit.,* and Atkins, *op. cit.,* p. 108 ff.

bizarre doctrine that "this world is not a solid sphere with humanity living on the outside, but a hollow ball, 8,000 miles in diameter, with men living on the inside." [40] An insistence on the flatness of the earth is one characteristic of another of these small sects, the Christian Catholic Church. This denomination, founded by the ex-minister and faith healer, John A. Dowie, who styled himself "Elijah III," erected for its believers Zion City, Ill., where it still exists in expectancy of the Parousia.

[40] Clark, *op. cit.*, p. 183.

CHAPTER IX

THE TRANSITION TO THE 20TH CENTURY

INCREASINGLY with the final years of the 19th and the first years of the 20th Century, the supranational character of the Catholic Church was made manifest in America. The New Immigration brought millions of Eastern and Southern Europeans to swell the population of the United States. Among the newly arrived Italians, Slavs and Levantines were thousands of Catholics of the Uniate Churches: Italo-Greeks, Ruthenians, Maronites and others. To provide spiritual care for these Roman Catholics of Oriental Rites, in an American Church predominantly Latin, priests of these ancient Catholic Churches emigrated to America and established churches in the centers of Uniate settlement; one, later two, special dioceses were erected to serve the Uniate Catholics. While similar dioceses were not constructed for the many nationalities of the Latin Rite, national churches for Italians, Germans, Czechs, Slovaks, Hungarians, Poles, Lithuanians, French Canadians and other national groups of the New Immigration were founded in enclaves of these peoples.

The presence of these new immigrants tested to the extreme the assimilative powers of the Catholic Church in America. Once more, the Church proved adequate to the task. "Out of the bewildering diversity and the sharply conflicting traditions brought by an immigration from every Roman Catholic group in Europe and from several of those of Asia and Africa, a unified church was progressively developed and, when the obstacles are considered, with amazing rapidity." [1]

The unification of these cosmopolitan groups in a single Church was not, however, achieved without difficulties. Some Eastern Catholics feared the Latinization of their congregations in the United States. When Rome, to avoid possible scandal to members of the Latin Rite accustomed exclusively to a celibate priesthood, decided to ordain no more married men to the priesthood in the Oriental Rite churches in the United States, some Uniates, believing their fears to be realized, abandoned Catholicism and joined the Orthodox Churches. Other immigrants, particularly among the Germans, clung tenaciously to their national languages and customs. In American Protestantism, this nationalistic spirit has led to the formation of many national sects. The American hierarchy of the Catholic Church appeared the preserve of the Irish, and so insistent were the American bishops on the quick Americanization of the immigrants and their children that the leaders of the Continental Catholic peoples in America feared for the perseverance of their distinctive characteristics.

Their grievance received its most noteworthy articulation in a petition presented to the Holy See, in 1890, by the secretary of the German Archangel Raphael Society, Peter Cahensly, whence these nationalistic tendencies received the

---

[1] Latourette, *op. cit.,* IV, p. 253.

name of Cahenslyism.[2] This document asserted that the Church as constituted in America had suffered an enormous leakage of immigrants and their progeny, mounting to the staggering total of 16,000,000.[3] It suggested, to avoid future losses, the rather radical proposal to divide the Church in America into a number of quasi-independent churches based on the nationalities present in the United States. While Cahenslyism contained elements of great danger to Catholic unity in this country, the successful progress of the work of unification of the American Church deprived the movement of its strength before the outbreak of the first World War.[4]

This nationalistic trend, however, produced the only apparently permanent schism which the Catholic Church has suffered in its four hundred years of existence within the present boundaries of the United States. At the turn of the century, a number of disaffected Slav congregations abandoned Catholicism and embarked on a career marked by quarrels and violence. While some congregations joined a small sect of Old Catholic immigrants, the majority eventually established the Polish National Catholic Church of America. Even this minor group of schismatics has not avoided further schism; the Lithuanians in the sect withdrew and set up their own national denomination. The story of these minuscule sects is, like that of all American

[2] Mode, *op. cit.*, p. 481, reprints the gist of the petition.

[3] Cahensly later (1910) reduced his estimate of leakage to 10,000,000. That this later figure is completely untenable is shown by Shaughnessy, *op. cit.*, p. 231 ff.

[4] Will, Allen S., *Life of Cardinal Gibbons*, I, p. 540, affirms: "Cahenslyism was, perhaps, the most serious danger which has ever threatened the progress of the Catholic Church in this country."

Old Catholicism, "a sad record of schisms, personal rivalries and jealousies, depositions and counter-depositions, and other events that constitute a scandal to Christian unity and charity." [5]

While American Catholics were engrossed with the problems facing the Church in the United States, they were suddenly startled by accusations emanating from Europe. A mistranslated life of Isaac Hecker, the convert who had founded the Paulist Fathers, was the source whence some French priests deduced the existence of tendencies in the American Church to minimize essentials of faith and obedience in order to bring the Church into step with the modern world. The furor caused by these accusations, and possibly the existence of such tendencies in European branches of the Church, influenced the Holy See to issue a letter condemning such trends, which were grouped under the title of "False Americanism." [6] The surprised leaders of the American Hierarchy immediately acceded to the condemnation, but denied that this "Americanism" existed in America. Cardinal Gibbons' reaction was typical: "I sent the Holy Father a reply to his letter received February 17 on the subject of Americanism. After thanking His Holiness for dispelling the cloud of misunderstanding, I assured him that the false conceptions of Americanism emanating from Europe have no existence among the prelates, priests

[5] Clark, *op. cit.*, p. 205.

[6] Cf. Mode, *op. cit.*, p. 485, for this letter.

Corrigan, *op. cit.*, p. 276: "At this distance the thing the Pope condemned seems to have been more prevalent in Europe than in the land from which it took its name. When Pius X alluded to 'Americanists' eight years later, in his condemnation of Modernism, he was certainly speaking to Europeans."

and Catholic laity of our country." [7] A few years later, Archbishop Ireland could write from Rome: "The Pope told me to forget the letter on Americanism, which has no application, except in a few dioceses in France!" [8] While it may have had no immediate application to conditions in the United States, the Papal letter was, nevertheless, salutary. The Modernism which caused difficulties in several Catholic Churches in Europe and which practically ended Protestant orthodoxy in many of the sects was thereby isolated from the Catholic Church in America.

Among the home problems facing the Church in America was the question of the relations of capital and labor, an issue which assumed increasing importance as the 19th Century drew to a close. A crisis was reached in the case of the Knights of Labor. This, the major labor organization of the times, and one which had many Catholics in its ranks, had been condemned by the Canadian hierarchy. It is important to note that the Knights were not condemned because they were a trade union organization; although many church leaders of the times considered the trade unions devices of the devil, the principles of trade unionism were not in opposition to Catholic moral teachings. Due to the power of the rampant capitalism of the times, the Knights were organized as a secret society; and it was for this reason that the Canadian bishops, reflecting the perennial Catholic suspicion of secret societies, condemned the Knights.[9] The liberal leaders of the American

[7] Will, op. cit., I, p. 557 f.
[8] Maynard, Theodore, Story of American Catholicism, p. 516.
[9] Commons, John R. et al., History of Labor in the U.S., II, pp. 201,

hierarchy appealed for a reversal of the ban, and Cardinal Gibbons presented to the Holy See a powerful plea for the Knights.[10] In response to the American request, the Papal Congregation of the Holy Office broke precedent when, by revoking the condemnation, it reversed a decision for the first time in its history.

Of greater and more lasting importance than this negative step was a positive declaration. A few years after the case of the Knights of Labor appeared the Papal Encyclical *On the Condition of the Working Classes*. This great charter of social justice demonstrated to the American people that the Catholic Church was vitally interested in the betterment of the economic position of the workingman, was fully aware of the problems produced by capitalism, and had a comprehensive plan to remedy its evil effects.[11]

The transition to the new century was not without its contribution to the history of bigotry in the United States. The American Protective Association, formed in 1887 to protect this land from the devilish machinations of Popery, gained some popular support when the Holy See appointed its first Apostolic Delegate to the United States in 1893.[12] The usual propaganda through the same well-worn canards,

338 f. The Church's opposition to secret societies was not new. The first condemnation of Freemasonry, for example, was issued as early as 1737, and has been frequently renewed. The history of the secret Know Nothings gives good reasons for this Catholic opposition to such secret groups.

[10] Cf. Will, *op. cit.*, I, p. 335 ff.

[11] Many Americans, and among them many Catholics, found—and find —the Papal teaching too radical. The original effect of this letter is illustrated by the Philadelphia Catholic who, on hearing the document read from the pulpit, rushed from the church crying "The Pope has become a Socialist."

[12] Cf. Myers, *op. cit.*, p. 219 ff.; Maury, *op. cit.*, p. 212 ff.

by apostate priests and "ex-nuns" as well as the publications of the bigot press, was issued. This later Nativism claimed at its peak over 1,000,000 supporters.[13] But it was pale stuff beside the bloody fury of the Know Nothings; there were but few riots and no murders. The major political parties hastened to disavow the anti-Catholics. After a futile effort to sway the Republican national convention of 1896, the American Protective Association sank out of the public view.

The transitional period saw the increase of Protestant efforts to regain the allegiance of the urban masses which had abandoned organized Christianity. Several instruments, designed with that end in view, had at once been diverted to other purposes. The Young Men's Christian Association and its sister movement the Young Women's Christian Association had been created to attract the proletariat, but they soon found their clientele composed almost exclusively of the bourgeoisie.[14] A revivalist campaign, headed by professional evangelists such as Dwight Moody and his colleague Ira Sankey, was aimed at the conversion of the lower economic classes; it succeeded only in regaining the allegiance of some lapsed members of the middle-class Protestant sects.[15]

A minor measure of success was attained by a few Protestant groups through the employment of other and

[13] Clinchy, op. cit., p. 89.

[14] Rowe, op cit., p. 144: "These associations adapted their methods to the needs of special groups, but they were middle-class institutions like the churches and they did not appeal to the lower stratum of the population."

[15] Schlesinger, op. cit., p. 13; Baker, op. cit., p. 90.

later methods, such as settlement work, community houses and "institutional" churches. These latter provided reading rooms, day nurseries, manual training courses and recreational facilities along with classes in religious instruction. By these means, some members of the urban proletariat were persuaded to join Protestant congregations. But their numbers were few. The statement of Latourette damns the efforts with faint praise: "Protestant Christianity did not wholly fail in the attack on the urban problem." [16]

Protestantism turned perforce to a study of the questions of social justice. Many ministers had awakened to the needs of the laboring classes and to the dire consequences of their apostasy long before the sects took official cognizance of the problems. These social-minded clergymen organized a number of groups, "The Societies of Christian Socialists," the "Brotherhood of the Kingdom," and the Protestant Episcopalian "Church Association for the Advancement of the Interests of Labor." [17] Members of these societies began the preaching of the "social gospel." This novel brand of religion was less theistic than humanistic; with some justice a Protestant minister has declared that, among the "social gospellers," "Religion is held to be nothing more than a plan of social well-being." [18] As it evolved, the "social gospel" taught the pantheistic concept of the immanence of God, and tended to abolish the existence of personal sin; it sought but a temporal salvation in the creation of an

[16] Latourette, *op. cit.*, IV, p. 370. Abell, *op. cit.*, p. 255, concurs: "But Protestantism had not solved the urban religious problem."

[17] Cf. Dombrowski, James, *Early Days of Christian Socialism*, p. 98 ff.; Hopkins, *op. cit.*, p. 319, *et passim;* Garrison, *op. cit.*, p. 152 ff.

[18] Quoted in Cole, *op. cit.*, p. 49.

earthly Kingdom of God.[19] For many years the devotees of the "social gospel" preached to deaf ears, for the domination of the sects by the middle and upper-classes long prevented any advocacy of the cause of the working-classes by bourgeois Protestantism.[20] It was not until the 20th Century that a Protestant movement for social justice became significant.[21]

In 1901, the Protestant Episcopal Church, by appointing a committee to study working conditions, was "the first Protestant denomination in the United States to take official recognition of the importance of the subject." [22] A few years later the Methodists drew up a series of resolutions on social problems which was adopted, in 1908, by the Federal Council of Churches and is known as the "Social Creed of the Protestant Churches." [23]

While Protestant interest in the social question was growing, the liberal Protestant theology continued its advance. The attention of all the denominations was attracted by several events, such as the heresy trial of Professor Briggs of Union Theological Seminary in New York.

[19] Hopkins, op. cit., p. 321 ff.

[20] Browne, op. cit., p. 421: "The more imperative task, that of asserting the pristine social doctrines of Christianity, went largely neglected. . . . The conservative quality, inherent in organized religion, buttressed here by the vested interests of many of the dominant religionists, proved an insurmountable barrier in the path of those who sought to make Christianity once more a gospel of social justice."

[21] Swift, op. cit., p. 115: "Although in the last quarter of the nineteenth century there were stirrings of protest against injustice and exploitation, it was not until 1907 . . . that the movement became significant."

[22] Fry, "Changes," p. 1014.

[23] Ward, Harry F., Social Creed of the Church, contains the "Creed" and an authorized commentary.

When Briggs was condemned as a heretic, his seminary retained him as professor of divinity, and severed its relations with the denomination which had ousted him.[24] In 1903, the Presbyterian Church, U.S.A., officially rejected the Calvinistic doctrine of predestination; and in the same declaration this quondam Calvinist church asserted the salvation of all who die before attaining the use of reason.[25] Orthodoxy was being driven to its last lines of defense.

The turn of the century did not pass without the usual crop of new denominations. There appeared several more Holiness sects with strange and sesquipedalian titles: Triumph the Church and Kingdom of God in Christ; the Church of the Living God, Pillar and Ground of Truth; the House of God, Which is the Church of the Living God, Pillar and Ground of Truth, Without Controversy.

In 1903 the fantastic "King Benjamin" Purnell established the bearded House of David. For a score of years, the "King" ruled his communistic colony autocratically and apparently used his power to rob his followers and debauch their young girls. When some discontented "Israelites" instituted a civil suit against their leader, the court discovered rather horrible conditions existing in the colony.[26] Purnell escaped criminal proceedings only by going into hiding for a period of several years; at the end of which he died. His small sect still exists.[27]

[24] Cf. Weigle, *op. cit.*, p. 223; Mode, *op. cit.*, p. 660 ff.

[25] For the text of the Presbyterian statement, cf. Neve, *op. cit.*, p. 332.

[26] Clark, *op. cit.*, pp. 193-195, reprints the findings of the court which occupy a page and a half of rather small print.

[27] For a fuller account of Purnell and his sect, cf. Ferguson, *Confusion of Tongues*, p. 56 ff.

Many of the new sects of the period can best be classified as "sacramental," for in contradistinction to Protestantism they maintained the full sacramental system of the Catholic Church. Together with the immigration of the Uniate Catholics had come many thousands of adherents of the Eastern Orthodox Churches. To provide for these, their national churches in the Near East established ecclesiastical organizations in this country. Thus a dozen or more new denominations were added to the already long list of American sects.

Another group of these "sacramental" sects may be traced to Joseph Rene Vilatte, possibly the most amazing ecclesiastical adventurer of the past three generations.[28] This Frenchman, after successively abandoning Catholicism and Presbyterianism, organized in the mid-West a group of Old Catholic congregations. The Old Catholics were a small body of European schismatics who, leaving the Catholic Church in protest against the decrees of the Vatican Council, immediately showed their devotion to the "purer" Catholic faith by repealing the laws of fast and abstinence, clerical celibacy and auricular confession. The European Old Catholics obtained episcopal orders from an older schismatic group, the Jansenist Church in Holland.[29] The original Old Catholics in this country were disaffected Belgian and French immigrants; later individual accretions

[28] Cf. Clark, op. cit., p. 206 ff.
[29] The Jansenist Church had been in existence as far back as 1724. After the Vatican Council, it threw in its lot with the new Old Catholics. Cf. Messenger, Ernest C., The Reformation, the Mass and the Priesthood, II, p. 610 ff.

came from the ranks of disgruntled Catholics and Episcopalians.[30]

After flirting with the Episcopalians and Russian Orthodox in this country, and the Jansenists and Old Catholics
of Europe, Vilatte finally received episcopal ordination on
the island of Ceylon from a bishop of the Thomas Christians of Malabar under instructions from the heterodox
Jacobite Patriarch of Antioch, in 1892. In 1898 Vilatte
suddenly abandoned his church and submitted to Rome.
He was shipped off to meditate on his transgressions in an
Irish monastery. When enough time had elapsed to indicate
that he was not going to assume high office in the Church,
he revoked his recantation and returned to reassume his
position as Archbishop and Primate of the Old Catholics
in the United States. Part of his following was lost to a
rival Old Catholic bishop with the resounding title of
Prince and Duke de Landas Berghes et de Rache. After
giving episcopal orders to a number of new sects, including
the short-lived Swedish Orthodox Church, and the strange
African Orthodox Church which was founded in Harlem
and soon had two schisms in Brooklyn, Vilatte once more
submitted to Rome and finally died in a French monastery.

[30] While at least one Old Catholic Archbishop and Primate was an
apostate Roman Catholic priest, an early Old Catholic schism from Vilatte's
group was led by a man who had been Episcopalian bishop-elect of
Oregon.

CHAPTER X

THE END OF PROTESTANT CREEDS

THE recent history of Protestantism in the United States is particularly noteworthy for two major developments. The first is the final abandonment of the older Protestant orthodoxy, in some instances by the official declarations of the sects. The second, to which the jettisoning of the Protestant creeds contributed, is an ecumenical movement which aims at the consolidation of all denominations in a single church and which has already effected mergers of a number of Protestant denominations.

The rejection of Protestant dogma was the culmination of the latest struggle between orthodox and liberal Protestants for control of the sects. This last phase began with the issuance, in 1910, of the orthodox publications *The Fundamentals,* whence the orthodox received the new name of Fundamentalists.[1] *The Fundamentals* was a series of twelve books published at the expense of two Protestant laymen who distributed, free of charge, 3,000,000 copies of the volumes to ministers and lay leaders throughout the world. The series stressed five basic doctrines, the chosen field of battle of the orthodox. These fundamentals are:

[1] Cf. Cavert and van Dusen, *op. cit.,* p. 65 ff.; p. 174 ff.; Beardsley, *History of Christianity,* p. 232 ff.

1. The inerrancy and divine authorship of Holy Writ;
2. The Divinity of Christ;
3. His Virgin Birth and Physical Resurrection;
4. His Substitutionary Atonement;
5. His Imminent Second Coming.

The fifth Fundamental indicates the sources whence the orthodox drew their main support. Since the millennial doctrine is typical of the sects of the lower economic classes, the bulk of Fundamentalist numbers came from the ranks of the poorer and less educated Protestants. Since the masses in the large cities are either Catholic or non-Christian, the Fundamentalists were dominant only in the rural areas and in the smaller towns. Their supporters were found chiefly in the "Bible Belt," the mid-Western and Southern strongholds of Evangelicalism, where the evolution of the Methodist, Baptist and other Evangelical congregations into churches of the middle-class had, chiefly for economic reasons, lagged behind the development of the urban congregations of the same sects.

Members of the opposition, now named Modernists, were not loath to accept the proffered gage. They agreed with the orthodox that the five Fundamentals were truly a "Great Divide." [2] Protestants of all denominations were to be judged by their acceptance or rejection of the Fundamentalist dogmas. The Modernists recruited their forces, as was to be expected, chiefly from the members of the upper and middle-classes, mainly in the urban areas of the

[2] Neve, *op. cit.*, p. 610, sums up the Modernist viewpoint, and not unjustly: "To Modernism, Christianity is essentially a kind of natural ethics."

country, and mostly from the older and non-Evangelical denominations.

The outcome of the Fundamentalist versus Modernist struggle, however, was determined before it began. By the beginning of the 20th Century, all vital faith had fled the formularies of Protestantism. The creeds were cadavers. There remained but the function of burying them. This the sects, over the futile fulminations of the Fundamentalists, proceeded to do. It was an honest act; but the sects perchance did not realize the significance of their action.

The first major Protestant denomination to take an official stand based on Modernism was the Congregationalist Church. At their national Convention of 1913 these lineal descendants of the Puritans officially rejected the necessity of belief in their creed as a prerequisite to membership in their church. The platform adopted by that meeting declared that conditions for church membership do not demand the acceptance of any special doctrines but have as their objective "the Christian life." [3] The Modernist position of the Congregationalists was further emphasized by the organic union of their church with the rationalistic Christian Churches in 1931 and by the establishment of fraternal relations with the once-despised Universalists. [4]

While the Protestant Episcopal Church still honors the official Thirty Nine Articles, the "comprehensiveness" sought by this denomination has permitted the growth of

[3] Neve, *op. cit.,* p. 499.
[4] Neve, *op. cit.,* p. 566: "The Universalists of today are in theology thoroughly Unitarian, largely pantheistic."

three distinct parties within that church.[5] The impact of the liberal theology widened the chasms between the sections, until in all save name the Episcopalians form three sects in one church. The Low Church party viewed with alarm the "Romanizing" proclivities of the High Church or "Anglo-Catholic" group and the Modernist tendencies of the Broad Church section; the Low Church reaction has been to assume a position scarcely distinguishable from that of some Evangelical groups.[6] The "Catholics" of the High Church faction stressed their ritualistic tendencies and equipped church edifices with confessionals, vigil lights, holy water fonts and other ecclesiastical furniture hitherto found only in Roman Catholic churches.[7] The Broad Church welcomed adherents of all varieties of opinion, "Trinitarians, Arians, Pelagians, Modernists, and sometimes out-and-out skeptics."[8] The Broad Church party "regards the church's formularies as symbolic of creative occasions in an expanding Christianity, and subject to change as human knowledge increases."[9]

In the years immediately following the close of the first

[5] Lyon, op. cit., p. 118: "The differences between these parties within the church is really greater than between them and the sects which stand for their fundamental tendencies."

[6] A typical Protestant view of these "Catholics" received enunciation in an address by the Moderator of the Presbyterian Church, U.S.A., to the Episcopalian convention of 1943: "Our church is committed to the principle of visible church unity, and never has sought to be merely a sect of the Holy Catholic Church."

[7] The Episcopalians offer an example of the trends found in all the sects by Browne, op. cit., p. 425: "The prevailing tendency was towards either a crypto-Catholic sacramentalism or a vituperatively evangelistical obscurantism."

[8] Neve, op. cit., p. 371.

[9] Cole, op. cit., p. 223.

World War, the orthodox throughout Protestantism assumed a more aggressive attitude. In Philadelphia, in 1919, they organized their supporters into an interdenominational "World Congress on Christian Fundamentals," and arranged that Fundamentalists seeking to regain control of their particular denominations receive the support and encouragement of orthodox of other sects. The Fundamentalist counterattacks of the Twenties, however, only hastened the rejection of the Protestant creeds.

The conflict between Modernism and Fundamentalism made a newspaper sensation of the famous "Monkey Trial" at Dayton, Tenn., in 1926.[10] In this celebrated case a high-school teacher was tried for violation of a state law forbidding the teaching of the theory of evolution in the public schools. When the Fundamentalists secured as prosecutor William Jennings Bryan, who since his political eclipse had become a leading figure in Protestant orthodoxy, and the Modernists retained as attorney for the defense the leading legal agnostic of the day, Clarence Darrow, the attention of the whole country was attracted to Dayton. Hundreds of newspapermen flocked to the trial, which quickly became a trial of Fundamentalism versus Modernism. Though the orthodox were successful in attaining a verdict against the teacher, the enormous publicity did not advance the Fundamentalist cause.

Fundamentalists among the Northern Baptists sought, in 1922, to gain control of that denomination by forcing through the national Convention of that year an official

[10] Cf. Allen, Frederick L., *Only Yesterday*, p. 201 ff.

creed.[11] The liberals repelled the attempt. Modernist strength was further demonstrated in the Convention of 1926. In that year, that most fundamental and singular Baptist dogma, the necessity of baptism by immersion for church membership, was rejected.

In 1923, Fundamentalist groups in the membership of the Presbyterian Church, U.S.A., forced an issue which resulted ultimately in schism and the discrediting of the Presbyterian creed. The General Assembly of that year, dominated by the orthodox, brought pressure to bear on Harry Emerson Fosdick, a Baptist Modernist who was serving as the minister of the First Presbyterian Church of New York City. Fosdick resigned his pulpit. But the "Auburn Affirmation," a document condemning the action of the General Assembly and virtually rejecting the Westminster Confession, was signed by over 1,250 Presbyterian ministers. When later in the decade Princeton, the last of the older seminaries to remain in orthodox control, succumbed to liberalism, the Fundamentalists moved towards schism. In the early Thirties, some irreconcilables abandoned the Presbyterian Church to the Modernists and established the Orthodox Presbyterian Church.

Since Wesley's day, the creed of the Methodists had been expressed in the Twenty Five Articles which Wesley himself had drawn from the Thirty Nine Articles of the Anglican Church. Modern Methodists, in the General Convention of the Methodist Episcopal Church in 1924, rejected an affirmation of belief in these Articles or in any creed as a necessary prerequisite for membership in the sect;

[11] Cole, *op. cit.,* p. 69.

new Methodists were simply required to pledge a vague "loyalty to Christ." The domination of Modernism among Methodist churchmen was further illustrated by the merger, in 1939, of the Methodist Episcopal Church with the majority of the membership of the Methodist Episcopal Church, South, and the Methodist Protestant Church on a creedless basis. The new Methodist Church, according to Neve, "wants to be, and it is, the Broad Church of American Protestantism, with room for conservative Essentialists and for outspoken naturalistic evolutionism side by side." [12]

By 1930 the Fundamentalist agitation, save for the futile recriminations of the irreconcilables, had largely ended.[13] Protestantism had abandoned its creeds.[14] There remains in America but one major church which requires of its faithful full acceptance of its teachings; in the Catholic Church alone of the major denominations is heresy still punished by excommunication.[15]

Consequent to the abandonment of dogmatic theology came necessarily a tempering of the moral teachings of Protestantism. "Perhaps the most profound of recent modifications of the conventional ethical outlook within the churches are those having to do with family and sex

[12] Neve, *op. cit.,* p. 427. Methodist Fundamentalists were known as "Essentialists."

[13] Cavert and Van Dusen, *op. cit.,* p. 175.

[14] Lynd, Robert and Helen, *Middletown,* p. 355, noted that: "Virtually anybody can join a church simply by signifying his intention to do so, and once in, it is practically unknown for any one to be ejected."

[15] Brown, William A., *Church and State in Contemporary America,* p. 262: "In Protestantism discipline has fallen into almost complete abeyance. It is rare, indeed, to find a church member cut off from communion for any cause whatever."

ethics." [16] Many sects approved, by word or by silence, the
practise of artificial birth control. In 1930 the Committee
on Marriage and the Home of the Federal Council of
Churches stated in its official report: "Whatever the final
conclusion may be, the committee is strongly of the opinion
that the church should not seek to impose its point of view
as to the use of contraceptives upon the public by legislation or any other form of coercion . . ." [17] The practise
of the remarriage of divorced persons by some ministers
would appear in the eyes of a critic virtually to repeal the
Ninth Commandment.[18] Protestant churchmen took a
leading part in the advancement of other practises scarcely
in conformity with the older morality. Literature advocat-
ing the legalization of euthanasia, abortion and steriliza-
tion appeared incomplete without the endorsement of
Protestant bishops and clergymen.

As the sects modified moral standards and surrendered
ancient dogmas, the sect members gave up the practise
of religion.[19] More and more Protestants spent Sunday
mornings in bed, on the golf course, in an easy chair with
the comics. The Lynds, in 1936, found that the typical
Protestant congregation had not changed in the decade
intervening between their studies: "Here, scattered among
the pews, is the same serious and numerically sparse
Gideon's band—two-thirds or more of them women, and

[16] Douglass, H. Paul and Brenner, Edmund, *The Protestant Church as
a Social Institution,* p. 299.
[17] Quoted in Fry, "Changes," p. 1017.
[18] Lynd, *Middletown,* p. 114: ". . . a few religious leaders refused to
re-marry divorced persons."
[19] Douglass and Breuner, *op. cit.,* p. 293 f.

few of them under thirty—with the same stark ring of empty pews 'down front'." [20]

These developments in Protestantism assisted the movement towards reunion which plays so large a part in the record of contemporary Protestantism. The continual emergence of schisms and the perennial crop of new sects had long since aroused the indignation and the apprehensions of Protestant churchmen. The call for reunion was heard throughout the 19th Century; it was taken up and intensified by ever larger numbers of Protestants as the years passed and the numbers of denominations grew. Today the leaders, if not the members, of almost all the greater Protestant sects are eager for opportunities to amalgamate their churches.

Other factors contributed to the growth of this ecumenical movement. Interdenominational social work and community churches, intercredal missions and theological seminaries, and interfaith church services, fostering an "open pulpit" and an "open communion," added to the example of the mergers of some denominations, fostered the trend towards Protestant consolidations.

While 19th Century efforts had little success in accomplishing organic unions between sects, several cooperative organizations short of union and preparatory to it were successfully established late in the century. Prominent among these bodies was the New York City Federation of Churches, founded in 1895. Within a few years, this group had numerous imitators, which in 1901 united in a National Federation of Churches and Christian Workers.

[20] Lynd, *Middletown in Transition*, p. 297.

From this body arose, in 1908, the Federal Council of Churches of Christ in America which grew until, in 1944, it contained twenty-five of the largest denominations in the United States, with an estimated membership of 26,000,000.

Other organizations fostered the growth of the ecumenical movement. Among these interdenominational bodies may be mentioned the Foreign Missions Conference of North America, which was created in 1893 and which was aided by the Laymen's Missionary Movement initiated in 1906; the United Home Missions Council set up by the Federal Council of Churches in 1908; the Christian Unity Federation established in 1910 among the Episcopalians and later opened to all Protestants.

Nor was the ecumenical movement restricted exclusively to American Protestantism. Protestant leaders throughout the world sought the reunion of shattered Protestantism. Several conferences of church leaders drawn from all the Protestant nations of the world met in Stockholm, Lausanne, Oxford and Edinburgh during the course of the Twenties and Thirties. These ecumenical conferences were attended also by delegates from the Eastern Orthodox Churches, for the leaders of the movement desired the eventual union of Protestantism and Orthodoxy. While the results of these ecumenical conferences have not fulfilled all the expectations of the Protestant leaders and the second World War has temporarily prevented further councils, a World Council of Churches has been outlined and continuance committees have carried on the work of the conferences.

Within the United States a number of organic unions

have been achieved. In 1906 part of the Cumberland Presbyterian Church merged with the Presbyterian Church,
U.S.A. Most of the unions since accomplished have followed the pattern of this amalgamation. They are consolidations of sects which once constituted a single church,
reunions rather than unions; part of one group usually
refuses to accede to the union and continues as a distinct
sect; the sects must be prepared to compromise on tenets or
practises unacceptable to the partners in the unions. The
Presbyterian Church, encouraged with this initial success,
established, in 1910, a Permanent Committee on Cooperation and Union with the express purpose of seeking unions
with other denominations; the example of the Presbyterians
was quickly followed by many of the major denominations. The Presbyterian Committee achieved its first success
in 1920 when its church organization was joined by the
Welsh Calvinistic Methodist Church, a small body which,
despite its name, was Presbyterian, not Methodist.

The fourth centenary of the Protestant Revolt was
marked by a movement towards reunion among the
Lutherans. In 1917 three Norwegian synods formed the
Norwegian Lutheran Church, and the General Synod of
the Lutheran Church, which in the 19th Century had
broken into three sects, was reconstituted under the title
of the United Lutheran Church. A dozen years later several mid-Western synods merged to form the American
Lutheran Church.

Even the Baptists achieved a partial reunion in 1911,
when some Free Baptists of Arminian provenance joined
the formerly Calvinistic Northern Baptist Convention. In

1922 the Evangelical Church was reunited to the United Evangelical Church; in 1940 this denomination consummated a union with the (German) Reformed Church in the United States, which in turn had been joined by part of the Hungarian Reformed Church in 1924. In 1931 the Congregationalist Church, which had added to its numbers some members of the Evangelical Protestant Church in 1924, formed a union with the General Convention of the Christian Church under the title of the Congregational-Christian Church.

The year 1939 witnessed the most important and the largest of all mergers—again a reunion—when the Methodists North and South healed the breach effected by the problem of slavery and were joined by an earlier schism, the Methodist Protestant Church. While a small group continued the independent existence of the Methodist Episcopal Church, South, and a remnant of the Methodist Protestants has established the Bible Protestant Church, this amalgamation of about 7,000,000 Methodists made the new Methodist Church by far the largest single Protestant denomination in the United States.

While the ecumenical movement strove to diminish the number of Protestant sects, new minor religious groups appeared to swell the list of religious bodies in the United States. Hollywood, that haven of eccentric exhibitionism, has succeeded western New York as the "burnt-over" district. The most publicized of the multitudinous Los Angeles sects is the International Church of the Four Square Gospel, founded and autocratically governed by the colorful "Maid of Angelus," Mrs. Aimee Kennedy

Semple McPherson.[21] In Hollywood also was established the American branch of possibly the wierdest modern sect, the Liberal Catholic Church. This minuscule denomination is a strange syncretism with episcopal orders from the English Old Catholics, a pantheistic theology based on Indian theosophy, and a membership open to all, including agnostics.[22]

The Liberal Catholic Church is but one example of the many sacramentarian sects which have appeared in the United States since the first World War. In 1921 the African Orthodox Church, whose Primate and Archbishop had been consecrated by Vilatte, was established in Harlem and soon had two schisms in Brooklyn. Three sects with sonorous names and a handful of followers received episcopal orders from the Orthodox. These new denominations, the American Holy Orthodox Catholic Apostolic Eastern Church, the Apostolic Episcopal (or the Holy Eastern Catholic and Apostolic Orthodox) Church, and the Holy Orthodox Church in America (Eastern Catholic and Apostolic), seek to unite Orthodox adherents in an American Orthodox Church using English as the language of the liturgy.

During the passage of the Thirties, newspapers made frequent mention of two groups on the extremist fringe of religion. The followers of Father Divine, a Negro mouthing sesquipedalian and meaningless words, can scarcely be called Christian if, as reports say, the adherents of this modern Messiah give divine worship to their

---

21 Cf. Ferguson, *New Books of Revelation,* p. 394 ff.
22 Ferguson, *op. cit.,* p. 279 ff.

leader.[23] The second group has been assailed as "the religion of the consciously second-rate which would never have gained a hold so strong had it not been for the underdog's superb sympathy with himself."[24] These Jehovah's Witnesses first appeared about 1879 under the leadership of "Pastor" Russell, who under the divine afflatus revealed that Christ's Second Coming was scheduled for 1914. When that year passed without the apparent advent of the millennium—unless one would call the first World War the Parousia—the "Pastor" announced that Christ's coming had been invisible. His successor "Judge" Rutherford, who had even less claim to the legal title than Russell had to the religious, added numerous accretions to the group. While the Witnesses had widened the assault on Catholicism characteristic of such groups to an attack on all organized religion, they constitute an inchoate Evangelical sect.

The latest United States Religious Census, that of 1936, indicated a most serious trend in church membership. While between 1926 and 1936 the "unchurched" had increased more than 10,000,000, the number of church members, although about thirty new denominations were reported for the first time, had mounted only from 54,624,976 to 55,807,366— an increase of less than 1,200,000. To only three major church groups were appreciable additions attributed: 1,310,000 to the Catholic Church, 550,000 to the Jewish synagogues, and 600,000 to the Negro Baptists.[25]

[23] Clark, *op. cit.,* p. 156: "This strange man is actually worshipped as a divine being by multitudes of people, as the author can personally testify, and he accepts this adoration as his right."

[24] Ferguson, *Confusion of Tongues,* p. 88.

[25] According to Fry, "Changes," p. 1024, the Jewish figures are not too

Prescinding from these three denominations, therefore, church membership, in spite of the addition of numerous new sects, had dropped over a million and a quarter. With the exception of the Lutheran synods, practically all the major Protestant denominations reported a decreased membership. In some large sects, losses exceeded 10 per-cent of total membrship. While the Presbyterian Church, U.S.A., the Protestant Episcopal Church, the Disciples of Christ, the Churches of Christ and the Negro Methodist sects lost over 100,000 adherents each, the Southern Baptist Convention is debited with a shrinkage in church membership of more than 725,000 and the white Methodist churches are reported to have lost about 1,000,000 believers.[26] It would appear that Protestantism, having abandoned its ancient faith, was being deserted by its faithful.

reliable, "because this denomination recently expanded its definition of a 'member' until its new membership figures are now virtually population estimates." Similarly, Mays and Nicholson, *op. cit.,* p. 12, write of the colored churches: "There is a desire on the part of denominations to swell their numbers, both with respect to churches and members. This urge to be 'big' in numbers is largely responsible for padded reports in church statistics."

[26] This trend may since have been reversed. *The Year Book of American Churches: 1943,* p. 148, reports a total church membership in that year of 68,501,186. The unreliability of the *Year Book* figures has already been noted.

CHAPTER XI

THE CATHOLIC CHURCH IN 20TH CENTURY AMERICA

THE tiny mustard seed which was the Catholic Church in the United States of 1789 has through the course of our history grown marvelously, until today it is a great and vital organism with deep roots and innumerable branches. Truly it is no exaggeration to state that: "In twentieth century America the Catholic Church, overtopping even the largest Protestant denominations, has become a power of unmeasurable importance." [1]

The status of the American Church as one of the great bodies of Catholicism was recognized by the Holy See early in this century. Throughout its long history in the British colonies and later in the United States, the Church in America had been considered a missionary field, and as such had been under the jurisdiction of the Roman Congregation of the Propagation of the Faith. In 1908 the Church in America was removed from the control of that body and accorded equal status with the ancient Church in Europe.

The great numbers and the continued growth of the church in the United States justified the action of the Holy

[1] Gabriel, *op. cit.*, p. 55.

163

See. Since no accurate census of American Catholics has ever been taken, the exact number of Catholics in any period of our past history will never be known. Estimates of varying reliability have been made for recent years. While the *Official Catholic Directory* for 1920 claimed 17,885,000 members for the Church in this country, the unreliability of the *Directory* statistics of church membership has already been pointed out. It appears more likely that in 1920 Catholics in the United States numbered about 20,000,000— about 20 per-cent of the total population.[2] Natural increase and the accretion of converts would have brought this number in 1930 to approximately 23,000,000, and in 1940 to about 26,500,000.[3]

Though the first World War and its aftermath, the new immigration laws and the great depression of 1929 dried up the source whence the Church had drawn large numbers of its faithful, membership in the Catholic Church has steadily mounted. While natural increase accounts for the majority of Catholic additions to church membership, an increasingly important source of new Catholics has been tapped in recent years.

Throughout its early history in the United States the Church had received a steady trickle of converts. Beginning with the 20th Century, the trickle has become an ever- increasing stream. The recent movement into the Church can

[2] Garrison, *op. cit.*, p. 197. Shaughnessy, *op. cit.*, p. 197 ff. The author cites on pages 211 and 213 two estimates of 1920 Catholic church membership by non-Catholics. The first, by a government statistician, is 23,000,000; the second, by a former member of the Census Bureau, places the numbers of Catholics in 1920 between 22,500,000 and 34,000,000.

[3] Garrison, *loc. cit.*, estimates 23,000,000 Catholic church members in 1930.

be compared to the frontier march into the Evangelical Protestant sects, but with some notable differences. The movement is not as striking, nor proportionately as large; and converts are not accepted into the Catholic Church on the strength of a sudden emotional orgy, but only after a period of instruction, which at times extends to a year. Nor is the convert accepted as a church member on the vague pledge of "loyalty to Christ," but only after he has given full intellectual assent to the entire body of Catholic dogmatic teaching. Yet in spite of these rigid demands of the Catholic Faith—the more rigorous when contrasted with the standards obtaining among the Protestant denominations— the numbers of converts have continued to increase. In the decade ending in 1930, about 300,000 adult Americans entered the Catholic Church. The following ten years witnessed a movement of over 500,000 new converts into Catholicism, while in the early years of the Forties the Catholic Church in the United States annually welcomed over 75,000 new converts.[4]

Many of these new Catholics have greatly assisted the labors of the American Church. While a large number of the most remarkable American congregations of sisters have been founded by devoted convert women, many of

[4] While Catholic pastors may over or underestimate the numbers of their parishioners, the Canon Law of the Church obliges them, under stringent penalties, to keep an accurate record of all baptisms. An annual tally of adult baptisms entered in parochial Baptism Registers would give, therefore, a quite accurate number of the converts of each year. Since the statistics of converts in the *Official Catholic Directory* are based ultimately on these accurate Registers, these *Directory* figures are clearly possessed of a higher degree of credibility than the church membership statistics of the same volume. The figures in the text are based on these *Directory* reports.

the hundreds of former Protestant ministers converted to Catholicism have become priests, some have mounted episcopal thrones, and several have founded noted congregations of religious men.[5]

In spite of the acceptance of the Catholic Church by increasing numbers of Americans, the traditional anti-Catholicism of the United States proved in the Twenties to have been not dead but dormant. The years immediately following the first World War witnessed a recurrence of Nativism, inspired by the Ku Klux Klan with its platform of "100 per-cent Americanism" and its violent attacks on Catholics, Negroes, Jews and aliens. The Klan leaders gained the support of amazing numbers of bigots throughout the country, particularly in the "Bible Belt" of the mid-West and South. Even in its heyday, however, the Klan perpetrated few notable acts of violence; the Klansmen expended their physical energies in wearing bed-sheets and burning crosses.[6]

But in the political sphere the Klan proved a dangerous enemy to American principles as well as to Catholicism. Early Klan attacks on the Catholic parochial schools achieved some measure of success. Alabama, in 1919, passed a convent inspection law.[7] And Michigan, in 1920, and again in 1924 barely avoided the enactment of an amend-

[5] Scannell-O'Neill, D. J., *Distinguished Converts to Rome in America,* lists 373 converted ministers. This compilation is incomplete, and the book, published in 1907, is long out of date. It is interesting to note that two converts sacrificed Episcopalian bishoprics in this country to become Catholic laymen.

[6] Cf. Myers, *op. cit.,* p. 282 ff.; Maury, *op. cit.,* p. 271 ff.; Ferguson, *New Books of Revelation,* p. 251 ff.

[7] Gabel, *op. cit.,* p. 485.

ment to its state constitution which was aimed at the destruction of the Catholic schools. Oregon, in 1922, enacted, in order to root out the Catholic school system, a law requiring the attendance of all school children at the public schools. The Catholic parochial school system, however, was saved and the bigots rebuked by the action of the United States Supreme Court in declaring the Oregon law unconstitutional.[8]

A final burst of Klan fury swelled up when, in 1928, the Democratic party became the first political organization in American history to nominate a Catholic for the Presidency. Klan propaganda, on a par in quantity and quality with the best efforts of the Protestant crusade of the 1840's, flooded the country. A recent author comments, "For pure virulence, there was nothing in all American history to equal the whispering campaign inaugurated against Al Smith."[9] In the subsequent election, the Democratic "Solid South," which was also a stronghold of the Klan, was shattered for the first time since the Civil War. While it is difficult to determine the effect of the No Popery propaganda on the election, the anti-Catholicism stirred up by the Klan unquestionably contributed to the defeat of the Catholic candidate.

This vicious electioneering was the last important effort of the Klansmen. With the advent of the great depression, this latest major Nativist movement, after a decade of influence on many phases of American life, passed into oblivion.

[8] *Pierce v. Society of Sisters*, p. 268 U.S. 510 (1925).
[9] Stone, Irving, *They Also Ran*, p. 301.

Increasingly as the 20th Century advanced, the Catholic Church assumed an ever more unique position among the churches of the United States. Amid the stresses and strains of the American environment, the Church alone of the major denominations remained true to the essentials of its foundation. While the opinions of the sects varied with the vagaries of public feeling, the Catholic Church continued to affirm its changeless moral and dogmatic doctrines.

Unique was the Church's position in educational and charitable work. In 1940 over 700 Catholic hospitals, 180 homes for the aged and 300 orphanages, besides other institutions, cared for thousands of unfortunates. In educational accomplishments the Catholic Church was without a comparable competitor among the Protestant denominations. While a half-million pupils attended Catholic high schools numbering 1,500, 2,000,000 children were receiving their primary education in 7,500 Catholic parochial schools. Only in the field of college and university education were the numbers of Protestant institutions comparable to those of Catholicism. The histories of these Protestant-founded secondary schools serves but to illustrate the profound differences between the two religious systems. While, in 1940, the two hundred schools of higher education founded by Catholics remained true to the Church and continued to teach the Catholic Faith and the Catholic philosophy of life, the situation was far different in the schools of Protestant foundation. Many of the Protestant colleges and universities had severed their connections with the sects which had established them; the great majority of these centers of learning are today not only non-denominational but scarcely Protestant, for they teach not a Protestant but a secular way of life.[10]

Unique were the efforts of the Catholic Church to solve the social and economic problems of the day. The Church has fostered the growth of organizations designed to put into practise the social doctrines it has long been preaching. A retreat movement for Catholic laymen has given spiritual instruction and assistance to thousands. Labor schools for employes and employers alike have been established in increasing numbers. Under the inspiration of the social teachings of the Church, Catholic trade union members have banded together to combat un-American social principles in their unions and to attack abuses and racketeering in union government and to bring the social doctrines of the Church to the attention of non-Catholic workers. Members of the Catholic clergy have instituted rural and urban credit unions and co-operatives. The mediation of Catholic priests is increasingly sought in disputes between capital and labor. A Catholic rural life movement has been gaining increasing attention. But the list of Catholic efforts in the social and economic fields could be lengthened interminably.

As we have seen, the history of the Catholic Church in the United States is the record of an unbroken advance. Losses, it is true, have been suffered, and mistakes have

[10] Garrison, *op. cit.*, p. 133 ff.

Cole, *op. cit.*, p. 40: "Most denominational colleges adopted the educational standards of secular learning and neglected the dogmatics of Protestantism."

been made. Yet, on the whole the chronicles of the Catholic Church in America present a record of which Americans interested in the spread of the Kingdom of God may be justly proud.

APPENDIX

LIST OF PROTESTANT SECTS NOW EXTANT
IN THE UNITED STATES

In the following catalogue will be found the titles of some of the Protestant denominations now existing in the United States. The names of some sects of more than minor importance are prefixd by asterisks (*). These denominations are again listed under the titles of their later national organizations, or under the names of the mergers in which they lost their independent existence.

The main sources whence this list has been drawn are: the United States Religious Census for 1936, the *Year Book of American Churches: 1943,* and the volumes of Clark, *Small Sects in America:* Lyon, *A Study of Christian Sects,* and Neve, *Churches and Sects of Christendom.*

PROTESTANT SECTS

Year	Name	Source
1607	*Church of England	
1620	*Congregational Church	Church of England
1628	*Dutch Reformed	Calvinists
1638	*Baptists	Congregational Church
1639	*Lutherans	
1640	*Presbyterians	Scotch Calvinists
1653	General Six-Principle Baptists	Baptists
1656	Quakers	Church of England
1671	Seventh Day Baptists	Baptists
1683	Mennonite Church	German Anabaptists

Year	Name	Source
1701	Free Will Baptists	
1717	Old Order Amish Mennonites	German Anabaptists
1719	Church of the Brethren (Conservative Dunkers)	German Dunkers (Baptists)
1728	Seventh Day Baptists (German, 1728)	Church of the Brethren
1734	Schwenkfelders	German Pietists
1734	Moravian Church (Unitas Fratrum)	German Pietists
1747	*German Reformed	Calvinists
1753	Associate Presbyterian Synod	Scotch Secessionist Calvinists
1754	Separate Baptists	Baptists
1774	United Society of Believers (Shakers)	
1774	*Reformed Presbyterian Synod	Scotch Covenanter Calvinists
1780	Free Baptists	Baptists
1782	Associate Reformed Presbyterians	Merger of parts of Associate and Reformed Synods
1784	*Methodist Episcopal Church	Church of England
1788	Presbyterian Church, U.S.A.	Major body of Presbyterians; broke in two, 1835; re-united, 1869
1789	Protestant Episcopal Church	Continuance of Church of England
1789	Universalists	Congregational Church
1793	Reformed Church in America	Dutch Reformed
1793	*Reformed Church in the United States	German Reformed
1794	United Baptists	Baptists
1794	Regular Baptists	Baptists
1800	Church of the United Brethren	Methodists
1803	Evangelical Church (German Albright Methodists)	Methodists
1809	*Synod of Reformed Presbyterians	Reformed Presbyterian Synod
1810	Cumberland Presbyterian Church	Presbyterian Church, U.S.A.
1812	Reformed Mennonites	Mennonite Church
1813	*Union Church of Africans	Methodists
1814	Reformed Methodists	Methodists
1814	Northern Baptist Convention	Major organization of Baptists
1816	African Methodist Episcopal Church	Methodist Episcopal Church

Year	Name	Source
1818	General Convention of New Jerusalem	Swedenborgians
1820	Brethren in Christ (River Brethren)	
1820	*General Synod of the Lutheran Church	National Lutheran organization
1821	African Union First Colored Methodist Protestant Church	Methodist Episcopal Church
1821	African Methodist Episcopal Zion Church	Methodist Episcopal Church
1823	General Baptists	Free Will Baptists
1824	*Welsh Calvinistic Methodist Church	Welsh Presbyterians
1825	Unitarian Churches	Congregational Church
1825	Duck River Baptists	Baptists
1826	Two-Seed-in-the-Spirit Predestinarian Baptists	Baptists
1827	Primitive Baptists	Baptists
1828	Quakers (Hicksite)	Quakers
1830	Disciples of Christ	Baptists
1830	*Churches of Christ (Christian Church)	
1830	Church of Jesus Christ of Latter-Day Saints (Mormons)	
1830	Primitive Methodists	English Methodists
1830	Church of God in North America, General Eldership	Reformed Church in U. S.
1830	*Methodist Protestant Church	Methodist Episcopal Church
1832	Reformed Presbyterian Church, Synod	The Synod of Reformed Presbyterians broke into these two sects
	Reformed Presbyterian Church, General Synod	
1835	Free Will Baptists (Bullockites)	Free Will Baptists
1840	Colored Methodist Protestant Church	Methodist Protestant Church
1840	Evangelical Synod of North America	Evangelical Church
1842	Amana Church Society	German religious communists
1842	Old Order Brethren (Yorker Brethren)	River Brethren
1843	Wesleyan Methodist Connexion	Methodist Episcopal Church
1844	Reorganized Mormons	Latter Day Saints

Year	Name	Source
1844	Mormons (Strangites)	Latter Day Saints
1844	Brethren of Christ (Christadel-phians)	Disciples of Christ
1844	Seventh Day Adventists	Millerites
1845	Evangelical Adventists	Millerites
1845	Mormons (Bickertonites)	Latter Day Saints
1845	Mormons (Cutlerites)	Latter Day Saints
1845	Methodist Episcopal Church, South	Methodist Episcopal Church
1845	Southern Baptist Convention	Baptists
1845	*Lutheran Synod of Buffalo	German Lutherans
1845	Quakers (Wilburites)	Quakers
1846	*Hauge Synod	Norwegian Lutherans
1846	Eielsen Synod	Norwegian Lutherans
1847	Lutheran Synod of Missouri	German Lutherans
1847	Apostolic Christian Church	
1848	Apostolic Christian Church, Naza-rean	Apostolic Christian Church
1848	Church of God (New Dunkers)	Church of the Brethren
1849	Union African Methodist Episco-pal Church	Union Church of Africans
1850	Conservative Amish Mennonites	Old Order Amish Mennonites
1850	Plymouth Brethren (Darbyites)	Eight small Evangelical sects
1850	Stauffer Mennonites	Mennonite Church
1851	Lutheran Synod of Wisconsin	German Lutherans
1851	Catholic Apostolic Church (Irv-ingites)	
1852	Mormons, Temple Lot	Latter Day Saints
1852	Congregational Methodist Church	Methodist Episcopal Church, South
1853	*Norwegian Synod	Norwegian Lutherans
1854	*Lutheran Synod of Iowa	German Lutherans
1855	United Zion's Children (Brinser)	River Brethren
1857	Christian Reformed Church	Reformed Church in America
1858	United Presbyterian Church	Merger of some Associate and Reformed Presbyterians
1858	Bohemian and Moravian Brethren	Moravian Brethren
1859	Church of God in Christ, Men-nonite	Mennonite Church
1860	Augustana Synod	Swedish Lutherans
1860	Free Methodist Church	Methodist Episcopal Church
1860	General Conference of Mennonites	Mennonite Church

Year	Name	Source
1861	Presbyterian Church, U.S.	Presbyterian Church, U.S.A.
1861	Advent Christian Church	Millerites
1861	Primitive Friends	Quakers
1862	New Apostolic Church	Catholic Apostolic Church
1863	Life and Advent Union	Millerites
1864	Christian Union	
1864	United Christian Church	Church of the United Brethren
1865	Church of God (Missouri)	
1865	Church of God, Adventist	Millerites
1865	Colored Primitive Baptists	Primitive Baptists
1866	Defenseless Mennonites	Old Order Amish Mennonites
1866	African Union Methodist Protestant Church	African Union M. E. Church
1866	*General Council, Lutheran	General Synod, Lutheran
1867	Social Brethren	
1868	*United Synod of the South	General Synod, Lutheran
1869	Reformed Zion Union Apostolic Church	African M. E. Church
1870	Central Conference of Mennonites	Old Order Amish Mennonites
1870	Colored Methodist Episcopal Church	M. E. Church, South
1870	Old Order Mennonites (Wisler)	Mennonite Church
1872	Danish Lutheran Church	Danish Lutherans
1872	Finnish Apostolic Lutheran Church	Finnish Lutherans
1873	Reformed Episcopal Church	Protestant Episcopal Church
1874	Colored Cumberland Presbyterian Church	Cumberland Presbyterian Church
1874	Krimmer Bruder Gemeinde	Mennonites
1874	Mennonite Kleine Gemeinde	
1874	Mennonite Brethren Church (Bruder Gemeinde)	
1874	Hutterian Brethren, Mennonite	
1879	Church of Christ, Scientist	Followers of Mrs. Eddy
1879	Jehovah's Witnesses (Russellites)	
1880	Salvation Army	
1880	Negro Baptist Convention, U.S.A.	Major body of Negro Baptists
1880	Church of God (Anderson, Ind.)	Holiness
1880	*United Norwegian Church	Norwegian Lutherans
1881	Christian and Missionary Alliance	Holiness

Year	Name	Source
1881	New Congregational Methodist Church	M. E. Church, South
1881	Old German Baptist Brethren	Church of the Brethren
1882	Brethren Church (Progressive Dunkers)	Church of the Brethren
1883	Reformed Presbyterian Church in U.S.	Reformed Presbyterian Church, Synod
1883	Mennonite Brethren in Christ	Mennonite Church
1884	American Rescue Workers	Salvation Army
1885	Missionary Bands of the World	Free Methodists
1885	Mission Covenant Church	Swedish Evangelicals
1885	Free Church of America	Mission Covenant Church
1885	Icelandic Lutheran Church	Icelander Lutherans
1885	Reformed Methodist Union Episcopal Church	African M. E. Church
1886	Unity Society	
1886	Church of God (Cleveland, Tenn.)	Holiness
1886	Church of God as Organized by Christ, Mennonite	Mennonite Brethren in Christ
1886	Church Triumphant	
1888	Churches of God in Jesus Christ, Adventist	Millerites
1889	Church of the Living God, Christian Workers for Fellowship	Holiness
1889	United Brethren (Old Constitution)	Church of the United Brethren
1890	General Conference of New Jerusalem	General Convention of New Jerusalem
1890	The Christian Congregation	
1891	Suomi Synod	Finnish Lutherans
1891	*United Evangelical Church	Evangelical Church
1892	Hephzibah Faith Mission Association	Holiness
1893	Daniel's Band	Holiness
1893	Independent Baptist Church	Swedish Free Baptists
1894	Church of Christ, Holiness, U.S.A.	Negro Baptists
1894	Burning Bush (Metropolitan Church Assoc.)	Holiness
1895	Christian Nation Church	
1895	Churches of God in Christ	Holiness

Year	Name	Source
1895	Church of God in Christ (Pentecostal)	Holiness
1895	Pentecostal Holiness Church	Holiness
1896	United Holy Church	
1896	Church of God and Saints of Christ	Holiness
1896	United Danish Lutheran Church	Danish Lutherans
1896	Church of God, Apostolic	Holiness
1896	Holiness Church	Holiness
1896	Volunteers of America	Salvation Army
1896	Christian Catholic Church (Dowieites)	
1897	Lutheran Free Church	United Norwegian Church
1897	Independent African Methodist Episcopal Denomination	African M. E. Church
1898	Finnish Lutheran National Church	Finnish Lutheran Church
1898	Divine Science Church	
1898	Missionary Church Association	Holiness
1898	Fire-Baptized Holiness Church	Holiness
1900	Apostolic Faith Mission	Holiness
1900	Lutheran Brethren of America	Norwegian Lutheran Church
1900	Holiness Methodist Church	Holiness
1901	Pillar of Fire	Holiness
1901	United American Free Will Baptist Church	Free Will Baptists
1902	Slovak Lutheran Synod	Slovak Lutherans
1902	Triumph the Church and Kingdom of God in Christ	
1903	Christ's Sanctified Holy Church	Negro Baptists
1903	House of David	Religious communists
1903	Evangelical Unity of the Bohemian and Moravian Brethren	Bohemian and Moravian Brethren
1904	*Hungarian Reformed Church	Magyar Calvinists
1906	Churches of Christ	Disciples of Christ
1907	Unorganized Italian Christian Churches	
1907	Pentecostal Church of the Nazarene	Holiness
1907	House of God, Which is the Church of the Living God, the	Holiness

Year	Name	Source
	Pillar and Ground of Truth, Without Controversy	
1908	Church of Illumination	
1909	Churches of Christ in Christian Union of Ohio	Christian Union
1910	Defenseless Mennonite Brethren in Christ	Mennonite Church
1910	Norwegian and Danish Free Church	Merger of Lutheran schisms
1910	Church of the Gospel	
1911	Assemblies of God, General Council	Holiness
1914	Churches of God, Holiness	Holiness
1916	Reformed New Congregational Methodist Church	Congregational Methodist Church
1916	National Baptist Convention of America	Negro Baptist Convention, U.S.A.
1916	Apostolic Overcoming Holy Church of God	Holiness
1916	Pentecostal Assemblies of the World	Holiness
1917	(Original) Church of God	Church of God (Cleveland, Tenn.)
1917	Pilgrim Holiness Church	Church of the Nazarene
1917	Norwegian Lutheran Church	Merger of Hauge Synod, Norwegian Synod and United Norwegian Church
1917	United Lutheran Church	Merger of Lutheran General Synod, General Council, United Synod
1918	*Lutheran Synod of Ohio	German Lutherans
1918	Free Church of God in Christ	Church of God in Christ
1918	Norwegian Synod of American Lutheran Church	Norwegian Lutheran Church
1918	Pentecostal Fire-Baptized Holiness Church	Holiness
1918	House of God, Holy Church of the Living God, Pillar and Ground of Truth, House of Prayer for All People	Holiness
1919	Father Divine's Peace Mission	

Year	Name	Source
1920	Holiness Church of God, Inc.	Holiness
1921	Congregational Holiness Church	Holiness Church, Pentecostal
1921	National Baptist Life and Soul Saving Assembly	
1921	National David Spiritual Temple of Christ Church Union	
1922	Evangelical Congregational Church	United Evangelical Church
1922	Free Magyar Reformed Church	Hungarian Reformed Church
1923	Pentecostal Church of God in America	Holiness
1923	(Tomlinson) Church of God	Church of God (Cleveland, Tenn.)
1924	Faith Tabernacle	Holiness
1924	American Baptist Association	Hard Shell Baptists
1924	Mt. Sinai Holy Church	Holiness
1924	Pentecostal Church, Inc.	Holiness
1925	Church of the Living God, Pillar and Ground of Truth	Church of the Living God, Christian Workers for Fellowship
1925	House of the Lord	
1925	Free Christian Zion Church of Christ	Churches of God in Christ
1926	Church of Eternal Life	
1927	International Church of the Four Square Gospel	
1928	Protestant Conference	Lutheran Synod of Wisconsin
1929	Kodesh Church of Immanuel	African M. E. Zion Church
1930	American Lutheran Church	Merger of Lutheran Synods of Ohio, Iowa and Buffalo
1930	Independent Fundamental Churches	
1930	Church of Revelation	
1931	Congregational-Christian Church	Merger of Congregationalist and Christian Church
1931	Calvary Pentecostal Church	Holiness
1932	Apostolic Methodist Church	M. E. Church, South
1933	Erieside Church	
1933	Church of God, Seventh Day	
1934	Christian Unity Baptist Association	

Year	Name	Source
1934	Evangelical and Reformed Church	Merger of Evangelical Church and Reformed Church in the U.S.
1935	Evangelical Baptist Church, Inc.	Free Will Baptists
1936	Orthodox Presbyterian Church	Presbyterian Church, U.S.A.
1936	Universal Emancipation Church	
1936	Latter House of the Lord, Apostolic Faith	
1939	Methodist Church	Merger of M. E. Church with major parts of M. E. Church, South, and Methodist Protestant Church
1940	Bible Protestant Church	Continuation of Methodist Protestant Church

OTHER PROTESTANT DENOMINATIONS—YEAR OF ORIGIN UNKNOWN

Primitive Advent Christian Church
Bible Presbyterian Church
Liberal Church of America
Evangelical Lutheran Jehovah Conference
International Pentecostal Assemblies
Pentecostal Assemblies of Jesus Christ, Inc.
General Council of Italian Pentecostal Assemblies
Unaffiliated Mennonites

International Ministerial Federation

Church Transcendant
House of Faith
House of Prayer
House of God

Church of the Open Door
Non-Sectarian Churches of Bible Faith
General Association of Regular Baptist Churches, North
Independent Lutheran Congregations

SOME INCHOATIVE DENOMINATIONS

Among the denominations to which conscientious objectors belong are catalogued, among numerous others, the following, taken from *Selective Service in Wartime: 1941-1942*, edited by Edward A. Fitzpatrick and published by the Government Printing Office, Washington, D. C., 1943, pages 264-265:

Ahtinsky Church
Biblist
Body of Christ

Bible Students' Ecclesia
Berean Church
Brethren and Episcopal

Christian Assembly
Church of Our Savior
Emmisaries of Divine Light
Kingdom of God
National Church of Positive Christianity
Peace Church
School of the Bible
Scientific Order of Spectrochrome Metrists
Zion Evangelical and Reformed
First-Century Gospel
Gethsemane
Gospel Tabernacle
House of Hosmon
Institute of Religious Science and Philosophy

Christian and Endeavor
Church of the First Born
Essene Religious Group
Moral Theist
Open Bible Standard

Peoples' Church
Truelight
Romanske Church

Fellowship of Reconciliation
Ukrainian Evangelical Pentecostal
Gospel Hall
God's Bible School
Immanuel Missionary

LIST OF BOOKS CITED

Abel, Theodore, *Protestant Home Missions to Catholic Immigrants*. Institute of Social and Religious Research, New York, 1933.

Abell, Aaron I., *Urban Impact on American Protestantism*. Harvard University, Cambridge, 1943.

Allen, Frederick L., *Only Yesterday*. Harpers, New York, 1931.

Andrews, Charles M., *Colonial Period of American History*. Yale University, New Haven, 1934-38; 4 Vols.

Andrews, Matthew P., *The Founding of Maryland*. Appleton-Century, New York, 1933.

Atkins, Gaius G., *Modern Religious Cults and Movements*. Revell, New York, 1923.

Bacon, Leonard W., *History of American Christianity*. Christian Literature Co., New York, 1897.

Baker, Ray Stannard, *The Spiritual Unrest*. Stokes, New York, 1910.

Bass, Archer B., *Protestantism in the United States*. Crowell, New York, 1929.

Bates, Ernest S., *American Faith*. Norton, New York, 1940.

Baudrilliart, Alfred, *The Catholic Church, the Renaissance and Protestantism*. Kegan Paul, London, 1908.

Bayley, James R., *History of the Catholic Church on the Island of New York*. Dunnigan & Bros., New York, 1853.

Beardsley, Frank G., *History of American Revivals*. American Tract Society, New York, 1912.

———— *History of Christianity in America*. American Tract Society, New York, 1938.

Billington, Ray A., *The Protestant Crusade*. Macmillan, New York, 1938.

Binkley, Wilfred E., *American Political Parties: Their Natural History*. Knopf, New York, 1943.

Boehmer, Heinrich, *Luther and the Reformation in the Light of Modern Research*. Dial Press, New York, 1930.

Bolton, Herbert E., *Rim of Christendom*. Macmillan, New York, 1936.

Bonham, John M., *Secularism: Its Progress and Its Morals*. Putnam, New York, 1894.

Bourne, Edward C., *Spain in America*. Harpers, New York, 1904.

Bowers, Claude G., *The Tragic Era*. Houghton Mifflin, Boston, 1929.

Brodrick, James, *The Economic Morals of the Jesuits*. Oxford University Press, London, 1934.

Brown, William A., *Church and State in Contemporary America*. Scribners, New York, 1936.

Browne, Lewis, *Since Calvary*. Macmillan, New York, 1931.

Buck, Paul H., *The Road to Reunion*. Little, Brown, Boston, 1938.

Carroll, H. K., *Religious Forces of the United States*. Scribners, New York, 1912.

Cartwright, Peter, *Autobiography*. Carlton & Porter, New York, 1857.

Case, Shirley J. et al., *Bibliography of the History of Christianity*. Chicago University, Chicago, 1931.

Castaneda, Carlos E., *Our Catholic Heritage in Texas*. von Broeckmann-Jones, Austin, 1936-42; 5 Vols.

Cavert, Samuel M. and Van Dusen, Henry P., *The Church Through Half a Century*. Scribners, New York 1936.

Channing, Edward, *History of the United States*. Macmillan, New York, 1905-25; 6 Vols.

Clark, Elmer T., *The Small Sects in America*. Cokesbury, Nashville, 1937.

Clark, Joseph B., *Leavening the Nation: The Story of American (Protestant) Home Missions*. Baker & Taylor, New York, 1903.

Clayton, Joseph, *Luther and His Work*. Bruce, Milwaukee, 1937.

Clinchy, Everett R., *All in the Name of God*. Day, New York, 1924.

Cobb, Sanford H., *The Rise of Religious Liberty in America*. Macmillan, New York, 1902.

Cole, Stewart C., *History of Fundamentalism*. Smith, New York, 1931.

Commons, John R. and Associates, *History of Labor in the United States*. Macmillan, New York, 1918-35; 4 Vols.

Corrigan, Raymond, *The Church and the Nineteenth Century*. Bruce, Milwaukee, 1938.

Coupland, Reginald, *The Quebec Act*. Clarendon Press, Oxford, 1925.

Dakin, Edwin F., *Mrs. Eddy: The Biography of a Virginal Mind*. Scribners, New York, 1929.

Davenport, Frederick M., *Primitive Traits in Religious Revivals*. Macmillan, New York, 1906.

Delanglez, Jean, *French Jesuits in Lower Louisiana: 1700-1763*. Catholic University, Washington, 1933.

Dieffenbach, Albert C., *Religious Liberty: The Great American Illusion*. Morrow, New York, 1927.

Dignan, Patrick J., *History of the Legal Incorporation of Catholic Church Property in the U. S.* Catholic University, Washington, 1933.

Dombrowski, James, *Early Days of Christian Socialism in America*. Columbia University, New York, 1936.

Dorchester, Daniel, *Christianity in the United States*. Hunt & Eaton, New York, 1895.

Douglass, H. Paul, *Church Unity Movements in the U. S.* Inst. of Soc. and Relig. Research, New York, 1934.

Douglass, H. Paul and Brunner, Edmund deS., *The Protestant Church as a Social Institution*. Harpers, New York, 1935.

Dunkerly, Roderic and Headlam, Arthur (edd), *The Minis-*

try and the Sacraments. Student Christian Movement Press, London, 1937.

Embree, Edwin R., *Brown Americans.* Viking, New York, 1943.

Ernst, James, *Roger Williams: New England Firebrand* Macmillan, New York, 1923.

Fanfani, Amintore, *Catholicism, Protestantism and Capitalism.* Sheed & Ward, London, 1935.

Ferguson, Charles W., *The Confusion of Tongues.* Doubleday Doran, New York, 1928.

—— *New Books of Revelation.* Doubleday Doran, New York, 1929.

Finney, Charles G., *Memoirs.* Barnes, New York, 1876.

Fiske, John, *Critical Period of American History.* Houghton Mifflin, Boston, 1888.

Frazier, E. Franklin, *Negro Youth at the Crossways.* Amer. Council on Educ., Washington, 1940.

Fry, C. Luther, *The U. S. Looks at Its Churches.* Inst. of Soc. and Rel. Research, New York, 1930.

—— "Changes in Religious Organizations." *Recent Social Trends in the U. S.,* II, 1009-60. McGraw-Hill, New York, 1933; 2 Vols.

Gabel, Richard J., *Public Funds for Church and Private Schools.* Catholic University, Washington, 1937.

Gabriel, Ralph H., *Course of American Democratic Thought.* Ronald Press, New York, 1940.

Garrison, Winfred E., *The March of Faith.* Harpers, New York, 1933.

Gasquet, Francis, *The Eve of the Reformation.* Bell, London, 1923.

Gillard, John T., *Catholic Church and the American Negro.* Josephite Press, Baltimore, 1929.

—— *Colored Catholics in the United States.* Josephite Press, Baltimore, 1940.

Griffin, Martin I. J., *Documents Relating to the History of the*

Catholic Church in the U. S. Amer. Cath. Hist. Soc., Philadelphia, n.d.

Grisar, Hartmann, *Martin Luther: His Life and Work.* Herder, St. Louis, 1930.

Guilday, Peter K., "The Catholic Church in the U. S." *Thought,* I (1926), 3-32.

——— *Life and Times of John England.* The America Press, New York, 1927; 2 Vols.

——— *Trusteeism: 1814-1821.* U. S. Cath. Hist. Soc., New York, 1928.

Hall, Thomas C., *Religious Background of American Culture.* Little, Brown, Boston, 1930.

Haroutunian, Joseph, *Piety versus Moralism: The Passing of the New England Theology.* Holt, New York, 1932.

Hart, Albert B. (ed), *American History Told by Contemporaries.* Macmillan, New York, 1897-1901; 4 Vols.

Hayes, Carleton J. H., *A Generation of Materialism: 1871-1900.* Harpers, New York, 1941.

Hooker, Elizabeth R., *United Churches.* Doran, New York, 1924.

——— *Hinterlands of the Church.* Inst. of Soc. and Rel. Research, New York, 1931.

Hopkins, Charles H., *The Rise of the Social Gospel in American Protestantism: 1865-1915.* Yale University, New Haven, 1940.

Hughes, Thomas, *History of the Society of Jesus in North America.* Longmans, London, 1907-17; 4 Vols.

Ives, J. Moss, *The Ark and the Dove.* Longmans, New York, 1936.

Jannsen, Johannes, *History of the German People.* Herder, St. Louis, 1906-10; 17 Vols.

Johnson, Charles S., *Patterns of Negro Segregation.* Harpers, New York, 1943.

Jourdan, George V., *The Movement Towards Catholic Reform in the Early Sixteenth Century.* Murray, London, 1914.

LaFarge, John, *The Race Question and the Negro*. Longmans, New York, 1943.

Landis, Benson Y. (ed), *Year Book of American Churches: 1943*. Sowers, Lebanon, 1943.

Latourette, Kenneth S., *History of the Expansion of Christianity*. Harpers, New York, 1937-45; 7 vols.

Loud, Grover C., *Evangelized America*. Macmillan, New York, 1928.

Lynd, Robert and Helen, *Middletown*. Harcourt, Brace, New York, 1929.

——— *Middletown in Transition*. Harcourt, Brace, New York, 1937.

Lyon, William H., *A Study of the Christian Sects*. Beacon Press, Boston, 1926; 13th ed.

MacLeod, William C., *The American Indian Frontier*. Knopf, New York, 1928.

——— "Contacts of Europe with American Aborigines," *European Civilization*, Vol. VII, 813-1062. Oxford University Press, London, 1939; 7 Vols.

McMaster, John B., *History of the People of the U. S.* Appleton, New York, 1883-1913; 8 Vols.

Maury, Reuben, *The Wars of the Godly*. McBride, New York, 1928.

Maynard, Theodore, *Story of American Catholicism*. Macmillan, New York, 1942.

Mays, Benjamin E. and Nicholson, Joseph W., *The Negro's Church*. Inst. of Soc. and Rel. Research, New York, 1933.

Mecklin, John M., *The Story of American Dissent*. Harcourt, Brace, New York, 1934.

Messenger, Ernest S., *The Reformation, the Mass and the Priesthood*. Longmans, London, 1936-37; 2 Vols.

Metzger, Charles H., *The Quebec Act*. U. S. Cath. Hist. Soc., New York, 1936.

Miller, John C., *Origins of the American Revolution*. Little, Brown, Boston, 1943.

Mode, Peter G., *Source Book and Bibliographical Guide for American Church History.* Banta, Menasha, Wis., 1921.

Myers, Gustavus, *History of Bigotry in the U. S.* Random House, New York, 1943.

Myrdal, Gunnar, *An American Dilemma: The Negro Problem and Modern Democracy.* Harpers, New York, 1944; 2 Vols.

Neve, J. L., *Churches and Sects of Christendom.* Luther. Lit. Board, Burlington, Iowa, 1940.

Nevins, Allen, *American States during and after the Revolution.* Macmillan, New York, 1924.

Niebuhr, H. Richard, *Social Sources of Denominationalism.* Holt, New York, 1929.

(various editors), *The Official Catholic Directory.* Kenedy, New York, annual.

O'Gorman, Thomas, *History of Roman Catholic Church in the U. S.* Scribners, New York, 1902.

Parkman, Francis, *Jesuits in North America in the XVII Century.* Little, Brown, Boston, 1922.

Parrington, Vernon L., *Main Currents in American Thought.* Harcourt, Brace, New York, 1930; 3 Vols. in one.

Pastor, Ludwig von, *History of the Popes.* Herder, St. Louis, 1906-30; 19 Vols.

Piette, Maximin, *John Wesley in the Evolution of Protestantism.* Sheed & Ward, New York, 1937.

Platner, John W. *et al., Religious History of New England.* Harvard University, Cambridge, 1917.

Ray, M. Augustina, *American Opinion of Roman Catholicism in the Eighteenth Century.* Columbia University, New York, 1936.

Rice, Madeleine H., *American Catholic Opinion in the Slavery Controversy.* Columbia University, New York, 1944.

Rowe, Henry K., *History of Religion in the U. S.* Macmillan, New York, 1924.

Ryan, John A. and Millar, Moorhouse E., *State and Church.* Macmillan, New York, 1924.

Scannell-O'Neill, D. J., *Distinguished Converts to Rome in America*. Herder, St. Louis, 1907.

Schlesinger, Arthur M., "Critical Period in American Religion: 1875-1900," *Proceedings, Mass*. Hist. Soc., 64 (June, 1932).

Scholes, France V., *Church and State in New Mexico: 1610-1650*. New Mexico University, Albuquerque, 1937.

—— *Troublous Times in New Mexico: 1659-1670*. New Mexico University, Albuquerque, 1942.

Sears, Clara E., *Days of Delusion*. Houghton Mifflin, Boston, 1924.

Shaughnessy, Most Rev. Gerald, *Has the Immigrant Kept the Faith?* Macmillan, New York, 1925.

Shea, John Gilmary, *History of the Catholic Church in the U. S*. McBride, New York, 1886-92; 4 Vols.

Shearer, Donald, *Pontificia Americana: A Documentary History of the Catholic Church in the U S.: 1784-1884*. Catholic University, Washington, 1933.

Silcox, Claris E. and Fisher, Galen M., *Catholics, Jews and Protestants: A Study of Relationships in the U. S. and Canada*. Harpers, New York, 1934.

Stone, Irving, *They Also Ran*. Doubleday Doran, New York, 1943.

Sweet, William W., *Story of Religions in America*. Harpers, New York, 1930.

—— *Religion in Colonial America*. Scribners, New York, 1942.

Swift, Arthur L., *New Frontiers of Religion*. Macmillan, New York, 1938.

Tawney, Richard H., *Religion and the Rise of Capitalism*. Harcourt, Brace, New York, 1926.

Thorpe, Francis N. (ed), *Federal and State Constitutions, Colonial Charters, and Other Organic Laws*. Government Printing Office, Washington, 1909; 7 Vols.

Tourcher, Francis E., *The Hogan Schism and Trustee Trou-*

bles in St. Mary's Church, Philadelphia. Reilly, Philadelphia, 1936.

Tyler, Alice F., *Freedom's Ferment.* Minnesota University, Minneapolis, 1943.

Vedder, Henry C., *The Reformation in Germany.* Macmillan, New York, 1914.

Ward, Harry F. (ed), *The Social Creed of the Churches.* Eaton & Mains, New York, 1912.

Weber, Max, *The Protestant Ethic and the Spirit of Capitalism.* Scribners, New York, 1930.

Weigle, Luther A., *American Idealism.* Yale University, New Haven, 1928.

Werner, M. R., *Brigham Young.* Cape, London, 1925.

Whipple, Leon, *Story of Civil Liberty in the U. S.* Vanguard, New York, 1927.

Will, Allen S., *Life of Cardinal Gibbons.* Dutton, New York, 1922; 2 Vols.

Woodson, Carter C., "Negro Slavery," *European Civilization,* VII, 553-594. Oxford University Press, London, 1939; 7 Vols.

INDEX

INDEX